# WRITERS' QUESTIONS AND ANSWERS

a&b

# WRITERS' QUESTIONS AND ANSWERS

Gordon Wells

First published in Great Britain in 2001 by
ALLISON & BUSBY Limited
Suite 111, Bon Marche Centre
241-251 Ferndale Road
Brixton, London SW9 8BJ
*http://www.allisonandbusby.ltd.uk*

ISBN 0 7490 5319

Printed and bound in Spain by
Liberdúplex, s. l. Barcelona

# CONTENTS

**Other Allison & Busby Writers' Guides by Gordon Wells**

*The Craft of Writing Articles*
*The Business of Writing*
*Be a Successful Writer: 99 Surefire Checklists*

**Also by Gordon Wells, published by Writers' Bookshop**

*The Magazine Writer's Handbook* (with Chriss McCallum)
*How to Write Non-Fiction Books*
*Writing ... is Fun!* (for children)

# INTRODUCTION

**What is the purpose of this book? What's it all about?**

At writers' conferences and get-togethers, at writers' circle meetings all over the country, and in the 'help' columns of writers' magazines, beginning writers all seem to ask the same questions. The answers to many of the questions are straightforward – once you know. Before you know, though, even the simplest problems can be worrying.

I don't pretend to know all the answers but after having been writing – and published – for more than fifty years, I have experienced many of the problems and found my way round them. For many years too, as 'agony uncle', I 'fielded' all the questions that the readers of the late, lamented *Writers' Monthly* magazine could throw at me. Throughout that period, when I didn't know the answer, I consulted someone who did. And all the time, I learned more and more.

The purpose of this book is to ask again as many as possible of the 'usual' questions and answer them as helpfully as possible within a single volume. Although there will undoubtedly be other questions that individual writers get stuck on, I hope the book can be thought of as a general 'Enquire within about the basics of writing'.

Get your answers here.

**How should I use this book? How is it organised?**

The whole book consists of questions – and answers. They are grouped together into broad areas of interest. There is a certain amount of duplication in the answers – I have sometimes judged it more helpful to answer a question fully, even though part of the answer might be available in response to another question or in another section of the book. Wherever appropriate, though, references are given to information elsewhere.

A beginner will find it helpful to read the whole book, straight through, from beginning to end. And then go back to specific answers as and when necessary.

And do not overlook the comprehensive index. (Every non-fiction book should have one.)

### The questions are fine – what about the answers?

I have tried to recall as many beginners' questions as possible, no matter how simple and obvious they may seem to an experienced writer. They worry a beginner and the purpose of this book is to alleviate as many such worries as possible. Many of the old *Writers' Monthly* questions appear in this book too – often generalised to ensure their relevance.

The answers? Well, they're the best I can come up with. I've been selling my writing for fifty years, I have had nearly 50 non-fiction books published, including a dozen for children, plus 11 children's novels and coming up to 20 book-length picture-stories – and I've given up counting how many articles. I have always done my own negotiating with editors and publishers, and I was, for many years, the editorial adviser for the Allison & Busby Writers' Guides. This entailed reading and reporting on every new Writers' Guide proposal put to them, and often guiding the work of those accepted.

Because so much of my own experience lies in the areas of non-fiction writing and a few narrow fiction areas, I have asked my good friend, Jean Saunders to vet my answers where they relate to mainstream genre fiction. Jean, who has written under her own name and four pen-names, has published more than 80 novels (in Britain and the United States) and half-a-dozen how-to books on writing. My thanks to her for this assistance – but the responsibility for any poor advice remains with me.

Whenever you've got a problem – dip in.

# FIRST THOUGHTS, FIRST STEPS

**Can a new writer break into the writing business – isn't it very much a closed shop?**

Possibly more than any other field of creative artistic activity, writing is open to anyone. Most editors – publishers' or magazine – will be only too glad to take really good work from a newcomer: a fresh mind with fresh ideas.

But those are the crunch points: the work has to be really good and the ideas have to be fresh.

Too many people who are keen letter-writers or who have written adequate management/technical reports at work, or frequently tell bedtime stories to doting offspring, think that they can write for publication. Writing for publication is a different skill. A skill that has to be learned. And too many people are not prepared to take the time to learn those skills.

Editors will tell you that 90 per cent of the material that is submitted to them for possible publication is totally unsuitable. Many put the percentage even higher. Is it really any wonder that they call the stack of unsolicited material 'the slush pile'? Any editor will tell you of their delight when they find a jewel in among the dross. But they know that most people submitting work to magazines and publishers are never going to make the grade.

Of course a busy editor will look first at work sent in by their 'regulars' – writers they can rely on to produce publishable material time after time. They would be foolish if they did not. They have to fill the pages of the magazine – or next season's book list. But they do also look – at first, perhaps cursorily – at the slush pile. And if anything looks at all worthwhile, they will look at it more carefully.

How do they decide if a submission is worth that second look? By the first few lines of a short story or article – the 'hook' – and the overall presentation. If it's a novel they will go a little further – read the first few pages and then dip in at random further on. If it doesn't grab them pretty well instantly, it's out. And if it LOOKS sloppy and amateurish – it almost certainly is. If it's a non-fiction book, it should be a proposal – and that's a different matter altogether – *see* Chapter 9.

So, back to the question. Can new writers break in? Yes – if their ideas and writing are good enough, if they act professionally, and if they work *real hard.*

**Am I too old to start writing?**

No. There is neither a maximum, nor a minimum age at which to start writing. There are many successful writers who didn't start until they were well into their sixties – maybe on retirement whilst a lot of writers start in their teens.

So, no more excuses, get to it.

**I'm just starting to write and I thought I'd try a few short story competitions. But isn't there a danger of my ideas being 'filched' by the professionals who judge such competitions?**

OK, there is no copyright in an idea. But I wouldn't worry about competition judges 'filching' your ideas.

First, they are likely to be far too professional to indulge in such plagiarism. Their reputation is too important to them. Secondly, they will be far too busy judging the competition – judging is difficult, time-consuming and, in my view, far from enjoyable, work – to sort out ideas that warrant 'filching'. And thirdly, even if someone did *lift* your story idea, their story would be totally different to yours. Indeed, it is often suggested to new writers that they take the 'taster' at the head of a published short story and write their own story from that idea.

Don't worry. Go in for short story competitions and good luck. Such competitions are often a useful way of getting your work noticed – the winner is usually published. And a competition success is probably worth mentioning when trying to break into a new market, particularly one which discourages unsolicited submissions.

**Where can I get help in learning to write?**

All over the place. There are books, magazines, evening and one-day courses of instruction, correspondence courses, writers' circles and workshops, as well as '*genre*-specific' national organisations that will help. There are also the marvellous – and most enjoyable – weekend or week-long writers' conferences and 'schools'. We'll look at correspondence courses in the next question.

I believe that a good book takes a lot of beating – and it costs less than a correspondence course. So … books.

For the absolute beginner, still unsure which writing field to venture into, these books are worth investigating:

*Becoming a Writer*, Dorothea Brande
   (Papermac, Macmillan, London, 1983 … and Harcourt Brace & Company/J. P. Tarcher, USA, 1934 and 1981.)
*Creative Writing*, Dianne Doubtfire
   (Teach Yourself Books, London, 1983.)
*Writing for Publication*, Chriss McCallum
   (How To Books, Oxford, England, 1989, revised 1997.)
*Writing Step by Step*, Jean Saunders
   (Allison & Busby, London, 1989.)
*Writing – The Hobby That Pays*, Gordon Wells
   (EPB Publishers, Singapore, 1993.)
   (Available only from the writer, c/o Allison & Busby, @ £8.50 post free.)

Getting into detailed instruction for specific yet broad writing fields, I suggest you have a look at:

*How to Write Stories for Magazines*, Donna Baker
   (Allison & Busby, London, 1986, revised 1995.)
*How to Write Short-Short Stories*, Stella Whitelaw
   (Allison & Busby, London, 1996.)
*The Craft of Novel-Writing*, Dianne Doubtfire
   (Allison & Busby, London, 1978, revised 1998,)

*The Craft of Writing Romance*, Jean Saunders
(Writers' Bookshop, Peterborough, England, 2000.)
*How to Write Crime Novels*, Isobel Lambot
(Allison & Busby, London, 1992.)
*The Craft of Writing Articles*, Gordon Wells
(Allison & Busby, London, 1983, revised 1996.)
*How to Write Non-Fiction Books*, Gordon Wells
(Writers' Bookshop, Peterborough, England, 1999.)

Apart from the above 'how-to' textbooks – all of which I know well, and heartily recommend as being written by successful British practitioners – it is also worth investigating the writing magazines. Most of these carry 'how-to' articles and columns and are all targeted at those willing to learn.

At the present time, leading British writing magazines are:

*Writers' News/Writing Magazine*: these two magazines are virtually 'joined at the hip' – if you subscribe to *Writers' News*, you automatically get *Writing Magazine* every other month. *Writing Magazine* is also available on the news-stands; the monthly *Writers' News* is not. Subscriptions (currently £44.90 per year, UK; £49.90 rest of world) to *Writers' News*, P.O. Box 168, Wellington Street, Leeds LS1 1RF.

*Writers' Forum*: bi-monthly, available from newsagents for £3 per issue, or subscribe at £18 (£25 for rest of Europe),for one year's six issues. Cheques payable to Writers International Ltd., to: *Writers' Forum*, P.O. Box 3229, Bournemouth BH1 1ZS, UK.

*The New Writer*: somewhat more 'friendly/amateurish' than the other two – 10 issues per year, on annual subscription only – £32.50. Write to P.O. Box 60, Cranbrook, Kent TN17 2ZR.

The leading American writing magazines are:

*Writer's Digest*: monthly – annual subscriptions $27 plus $10 surface post, or $56 airmail, from *Writer's Digest*, 1507 Dana Avenue, Cincinnati, OH 45207, USA.

*The Writer*: monthly – annual subscriptions $29 in U.S., $59 outside of North America. Write to The Writer Inc., 120 Boylston Street, Boston, MA 02116, USA.

Your local library will probably have details of local writing circles and further educational courses in writing. I would always, myself, go for something called 'Writing for Publication' rather than 'Creative Writing' which may not be aimed at producing work for sale.

When contemplating an evening (or day) course on writing, investigate the experience of the tutor. If they write only poetry, their course is unlikely to cover article-writing well – and possibly nothing commercial at all. If they are not published – whence cometh their expertise for teaching you? But if the tutor really knows his/her stuff, a course of evening, or similar, classes can be extremely valuable.

It is wise to make similar enquiries about local writing circles. Their value to you will depend on the 'senior' members – do they know enough to assist you? And avoid the circle that is no more than a 'tea-and-gossip' gathering. A busy, working circle is a joy; a lazy, chatty one a disaster.

The most prominent and helpful of the specialist national organisations is, without doubt, the Romantic Novelists' Association – the RNA. Unpublished authors can join – but are then required to submit a complete romantic novel each year to retain their membership. The submitted novels are reviewed by the RNA; those thought up to publication standard are forwarded to appropriate publishers by the RNA; the rest receive detailed and helpful criticism. Check the latest edition of one of the writing handbooks for the contact address, which changes.

There are also weekend and week-long writers' 'get-togethers' – conferences or 'schools' where *direct* help is usually available. Every new writer should investigate one or other of these events: participants are quickly immersed in the company of other writers – and most writers are willing to give generously of their time and advice to newcomers. The most important and best-known annual gatherings are:

**The Writers' Summer School** ('Swanwick'): a six-day annual event in August, held at Swanwick in Derbyshire. For all writers – beginners to top professionals. Usually has a choice of at least half-a-dozen five-lecture courses (including one for absolute beginners), ten 'main' talks (by big-name writers) and dozens of one-off lectures and discussion groups. (There is always a number of overseas visitors – including a handful of American 'regulars' – to the Swanwick week.) Contact the Secretary, Writers' Summer School, PO Box 5532, Heanor, DE 75 7Y F.

**The Writers' Holiday** ('Caerleon'): a six-day annual event in July, held at Caerleon in South Wales. Mainly geared to beginners. Participants can attend two five-lecture courses during the week – choosing from about eight – plus a variety of one-off talks and other activities. Contact D. L. Anne Hobbs, School Bungalow, Church Road, Pontnewydd, Cwmbran, South Wales NP44 1AT.

**The Southern Writers Conference**: an annual weekend in June, held at Earnley Concourse, not far from Chichester in West Sussex. Main speakers and discussion groups. Contact the Secretary, Lucia White, Stable House, Home Farm, Coldharbour Lane, Dorking, Surrey RH4 3JG.

There are several other excellent writers' gatherings – see notices in the writing press. To contact any of the above, always enclose a stamped addressed envelope.

**Of what value are correspondence courses to a new writer?**

The course material provided by correspondence courses is usually excellent. And many such courses introduce the student to a wide range of writing activities that they might not otherwise attempt. The real value of a correspondence course though, depends a lot on the individual tutor who deals with the student.

A good tutor, with the right sort of practical experience, can be worth the cost of the course many times over. A good correspondence tutor can help the willing student achieve repeated publication. A good tutor is someone sitting beside you, holding your hand as you learn. But of course, not all tutors are good. Some may be excellent writers but less able to offer the focused encouragement that a new writer needs; others may be pretentious small-achievers who could guide a beginner down a totally wrong road.

Another of the benefits of a correspondence course is that it 'makes' the student work – submitting exercises, reworking 'almost-theres'. We are all liable to procrastinate rather than get down to work. But even the dreaded tutorial assignments will only work if the students themselves are prepared to buckle down to them.

If you work well on your own, you may not need a correspondence course. However if you welcome being told what to do – and given a deadline – you may find a correspondence course is just what you need.

My recommendation would be to buy a how-to book first, to see if you can manage on your own. If not, investigate correspondence tuition.

**I know HOW to write – but I can't think what to write about. Where do the ideas come from – how can I develop my own ideas?**

I believe that writing for publication is a four-tiered process – and the writing itself, the joining together of words, is a relatively small part of the finished product. My four tiers – starting with the 'foundations' – are:

1. Knowing your subject and having an idea. This has to be a really hefty tier, almost worthy of separating subject and idea – but they are so closely linked I think them better dealt with together. Both are essential for a non-fiction writer, while the idea usually takes pride of place for a fiction writer. Subject research though is usually necessary for all writing.
2. Knowing the market place. Knowing who will take your work and what that market wants – the ever-essential market study.
3. Writing. Not *just* writing: producing an entertaining and/or interesting 'easy read'.
4. Presentation and marketing. Being businesslike.

You are right: ideas are essential. Sometimes, they come in a sudden flash of inspiration: make a note of them immediately – they can disappear in a flash too. But you can't rely solely on occasional inspirational flashes – you need a steady flow of ideas.

Let's consider non-fiction first. It is helpful to list all the things about which you have some knowledge.

# WRITERS' QUESTIONS AND ANSWERS

Writers are frequently advised to WRITE ABOUT WHAT YOU KNOW but I think that this is too restricting and would amend it to GET TO KNOW YOUR SUBJECT WELL BEFORE WRITING ABOUT IT. For now though, list what you already know.

Be wide-ranging, extravagant and immodest in your listing – no one's going to see your list except you. It's a working tool, not a CV. Most of us know about:

• past or present jobs, and/or hobby(ies)
• things we have done – even that not-very-successful DIY repair job
• places we have been – home or abroad
• subjects we are, or have been, interested in and read up on
• things we collect – or once collected
• one or two interesting people/personalities – everyone knows someone interesting, or who does or collects something interesting or has been somewhere unusual.

Purely as an example, my own immodest list would include: my jobs in England and Borneo; my work as an engineer, an administrator, a personnel manager, an author and a lecturer; my hobbies of writing and photography; my holidays in Russia, China and on the French rivers; my interest in dragons and English revolutions; my collections of seashells and Asian antiques; and my one-time neighbour who made miniature copies of big-band drum kits. As you can see, a complex and wide-ranging list – although, of course, I don't pretend to be an expert in many of those areas. And I'll bet that you too could produce an equally wide-ranging list.

Now, the ideas. First, there is a possibility that one or two of your listed 'knowledge-areas' could themselves work up into saleable articles. (I have sold articles about antiques, dragons, revolutions, job interview techniques, lecturing techniques, most of my holidays and any number of writing techniques. I have written books about traffic engineering, personnel management and writing techniques.)

Secondly – and potentially more productively – you can 'mix-and-match' from your list. As a photographer I have collected pictures of statues: putting this interest together with my interest in English revolutionaries, I have sold illustrated articles about their London statues. My interest in dragons led to a commission for a children's book about dinosaurs. Not quite 'mix-and-match' but the publisher thought that if I knew about dragons I ought also to know about dinosaurs.

Think too about what *other* people are interested in. Listen to other people's conversations – all writers 'earwig' – and take note of what they are talking about. In general, people are interested in their jobs, their hobbies, their relationships, their houses, their finances and their health. Not dissimilar to your own list? Now think about what, from your own knowledge and experience you can write that will appeal to the general public. Ideas will slowly blossom.

Another source of article ideas is to brainstorm. Pick a subject or an object – and repeatedly ask yourself questions about it. The start-up questions should be those dear to every journalist's heart – Who? What? Why? Where? When? and How? I remember them as 5WH.

Who invented that? What does it do/achieve? How does it work? When and where was it introduced? Why was it needed? And as you discover the answers to the initial questions, ask further similar questions to take your investigations deeper and deeper. Slowly, you will find yourself interested in that random subject. And if you are interested, surely you can interest others? As a writer, that's your job.

As well as the above ideas for developing article ideas, other sources are:

- other people's articles – old or recent – there's no copyright in ideas
- news-related items – but work fast or someone else will get there first
- proverbs, clichés, quotes, etc., used as titles – give 'em a twist to be different
- 10, 12, or 20 tips on How to …
- a target magazine's 'agony column' – if people are worried about something, maybe you can help them

With fiction, both short and long, the single basic generator of ideas is the question, What if …? Ask it often. Exercise your imagination and put your characters into strange situations and then see how they extricate themselves.

More specific fiction idea-sources – mostly for short stories:

- Read ONLY the 'taster' (or blurb) printed in bold at the head of a published short story. Write your own story to fit that introduction – don't worry, it will be quite different from the original one.
- Investigate pop songs – both present-day hits and all the 'oldies' – after all, they usually tell of requited or unrequited love and what more do you want for a romantic short story?
- Build on snippets of overheard conversation – you don't need to pick up much if you have a warped sense of humour and/or a lively imagination
- Take a familiar nursery rhyme or bedtime story and update it – e.g., the Three Little Pigs might be three brothers, each housed differently and the wolf, an unscrupulous property developer.
- Look for unusual characters – in the park, in the supermarket, on the commuter train – and speculate about their lives (Play What if …?).
- Again, as for articles – raid the 'agony columns' and the Letters page.

And, so important it bears repeating – once you get an idea, **WRITE IT DOWN**.

### Where do I find out?

We're still in that extra-thick bottom tier of the writing process referred to in the previous answer. Subject research. Don't be put off by the word research. A writer doesn't have to reinvent the wheel or expand the frontiers of human knowledge – merely to know, or find out, enough to give the reader something new.

Information is all about us. You just need to delve. Apart from the books on my own shelves – which are legion, see below – my first research stop is usually the local library. I always look in the children's section first. Depending on my reasons for researching, the children's section may meet all my needs. Beyond that though, there are the encyclopaedias and all the subject-specific books available right off the shelves or to order for a small fee. Your local library is one of your best sources.

But you will also gradually build up your own personal library of reference sources that are directly related to your specific interests. As I mentioned above, I am interested in English revolutions: I have about 10 feet (say, 3 metres) of shelf-space full of books about Britain's revolutionary past. I bought many of these from remainder bookshops – particularly Bibliophile or Postscript (*see* page 130). Their subject matter was too narrow to sustain a broad general interest, which made them exactly what I wanted, and explains why I got them for bargain prices.

Similarly, I have collections of books, built up over many years, about other specific interests – including traffic engineering, economics, Asia, dragons, management techniques and, of course, how-to books on all aspects of writing.

Of more general use and interest, apart from several children's books, I have a couple of single-volume encyclopaedias and two multi-volume encyclopaedia sets. I have a large handful of books of quotations – always useful for lightening-up add-ins to serious feature articles. Because I do a lot of mini-biographies for a children's magazine, I have several biographical encyclopaedias. And books that I find amazingly useful in all sorts of unexpected areas include a *Chronicle of the 20th Century*, the 'serious' date-related *On This Day* and Jeremy Beadle's amusing *Today's the Day*.

I find the CD of *Encarta* which came bundled with my computer more useful than I had originally expected; I'm sorely tempted to invest in the new 2-CD version.

Then there's the internet. In theory, you can research anything in the world via the World Wide Web: in practice I can often find just what I need more quickly from my reference books. But there are many areas in which the internet is superb. I don't believe in listing particularly useful web-sites as something better always comes along the moment I stop writing! Investigate the internet yourself: it's a great resource – when you get used to it.

But never forget the more ordinary research sources – your personal contacts. Individual people have amazing knowledge about all sorts of unusual subjects: all you need is to know which of your friends knows all about what.

For further detailed advice on research – it's written for novelists but is equally relevant for much non-fiction research too – *see* Jean Saunders' informative and readable *How to Research Your Novel* (Allison & Busby, London, 1993).

**Why do I have to do a word count? How best should I do it and how present it?**

You *yourself* need a word count; most magazines specify their preferred length of article and short story. If you don't do your own word count, you'll never know how close to that figure you are. The magazine too, to which you will be submitting your work likes to be told the length of your submission. Yes, they can estimate it, but they prefer it to be done for them – they'll check later.

You will find, in the chapter on writing style, that I recommend certain average and maximum lengths of sentences and paragraphs. I repeatedly check my sentences and paras against my own recommendation – using the computer's word count facility – and often trim down to match. If you don't count your words, you don't really know where you are; how your work is progressing. Indeed, John Braine, in his *Writing a Novel* says categorically, '… a writer is a person who counts words.'

Similarly with books, a publisher will want, or commission you to provide, a book of so many thousand words. Going over or under that specified requirement could damage the commercial viability of the book.

Too long a text will increase the unit cost and may require the list price to be varied. Too short a text and the resultant book may not *look* thick enough to warrant the economical list price. Publishers, cynically conscious that the public buys books by weight, can increase the weight of the paper – but there *is* a limit.

Your computer will count your words for you. This word count is ideal for my sentence and para length checks; it is likely to be incorrect when checking thousand-word articles or larger works. Some errors spring from the computer's custom of counting e.g., dashes as whole words. With an article or short story I would be quite happy to accept the computer count.

The computer will tell you that your article is 786 words long. That may include the title and byline, the line of dots at the end and possibly your name and address. Make allowances to the count for these extras. Do not specify the length to the editor as 786 words. Round it up or down – and adjusting for the title etc., I would probably call it 750 words. Under 800 words overall length, I would round the count off to the nearest 50 words. Over 800 words round to the nearest 100.

With a book, I would recommend that you use the computer word count by chapters, rounding each up to the next – i.e., NOT to the nearest – five hundred words. Then add the chapter word counts together to give a total book count. Rounding up will give a slightly generous figure but this doesn't matter. Publishers are interested in the number of book pages that the text will occupy, which include the blank bits at the beginning and end of each chapter. The rounding up and the blank spaces probably balance out.

You will also need to count words when investigating a potential market. You will be assessing the lengths of actual published work. Count a hundred words and measure the length of column that occupies. Next, measure the total column length and multiply up. A slightly less accurate approach is to measure the length of a single column, multiply that up for a standard column wordage – and multiply up by number of columns, making allowances for cross-heads, illustrations, etc. Be careful to check whether the columns change width from page to page. For published book lengths, count the words on a typical full page and multiply up.

## How can I find time to write?

Only you can answer that question but, if you want to be a successful writer, you've just got to find, or make time. Prioritise your activities: if watching the television is of more importance than getting on with your Great British Novel … then perhaps you shouldn't start it. The *real writer* can't not write: the *real writer* MAKES TIME to write.

One writing friend, with a demanding young family, used to get up at about 05.30; she wrote in blissful solitude for an hour a day before anyone else woke up.

When I was a wage-slave, commuting to London, I had to leave the house at 07.00 each morning – and got home by about 7 each night. I ate dinner and then wrote most evenings until 9. And I also wrote for several hours each weekend. (One does need a sympathetic partner to help with the housework, though.)

You will know your own circumstances: try to set aside a regular period each day for writing; if you only manage to write 300 words each day, you will complete the first draft of a good-sized 100,000-word novel in a year – or a couple of short stories per month or one article a week. Make your mind up.

**How long does it take an experienced writer to write a ... novel/non-fiction book/short story/article?**

This is an impossible question to answer – different writers write at different speeds. All that really matters is the quality of the final result.

As a piece of useless information though, I usually manage to produce about 300 words of near-finished non-fiction – article or book – in an hour, if I don't have to do much research while writing. In other words, writing about a subject I know fairly well – like many of the answers in this book. Some have been produced much more slowly though – where I have needed to consult reference material while writing. In the same context, when writing a non-fiction book about a familiar subject I often manage about 2,500 words in a 'full' day of writing.

In support of the Bernard Shaw apology – he didn't have the time to write a shorter letter – it always takes me longer to write a really concise, crisp article. A 600-word article could take more than half a day to write – and polish.

Some of my writing friends tell me that, when things are going well, they can start and finish a short story in one full day. Several *genre* writers assure me that they usually write about half a book chapter per day – say, 2,500 words. One such writer regularly produces a 5,000-word chapter per day – but, of course, she spends a lot of time thinking about the plot before she starts writing.

Against those examples, I also know a writer who can spend hours on a single paragraph – but sells all she writes, first time out. The late Dianne Doubtfire, in her excellent *Creative Writing* said that she was satisfied if she managed to write a thousand words – 'and cross out half of them' – in a six-hour working day.

A few relevant quotes:

Ernest Hemingway: 'Wearing down seven number two pencils is a good day's work.'
Evelyn Waugh: '2000 words a day is very good going.'
Anthony Burgess: 'I wrote much because I was paid little.'

And Anthony Trollope is said to have turned out forty-nine pages of manuscript per week – exactly seven pages per day, never more, never less.

So … don't worry about how fast or slow you write. Worry only about whether or not what you write is good enough to sell.

**Many fiction writers use a pen-name. Do I need to use one – and how do I go about it?**

Using a pen-name is a personal choice – you certainly don't HAVE to use one. The majority of writers write exclusively under their own name.

There are a number of reasons why some writers use one or more pen-names:

- For differentiation purposes. Their own name may have become 'established' in one genre – and they want to write in another. For example, if a well-known crime writer wanted to write a romance, they might well adopt a pen-name – to avoid confusing the fans of their crime books. A publisher might require the use of a pen-name in such a situation. Another reason for differentiation might be to distinguish between 'heavy' non-fiction books and lightweight fiction.
- To avoid appearing too prolific. A second series of books, under a different name, might attract a whole new batch of fans.
- For contractual reasons – to work with a different publisher. The 'next book' clause in an Agreement can sometimes be an unwelcome tie – often, again, due to a prolific output – and a pen-name can be a useful compromise.
- To suit the *genre*. Some *genres* seem to require authors of a particular sex: e.g., most romances are written by women, most Westerns by men. A 'branching-out' writer will often adopt a different sex pen-name to suit the 'new' *genre*. Even Phyllis James writes her crime novels as P. D. James.
- To avoid embarrassment – which is probably the least valid reason for adopting a pen-name. Why should you not want others to know about your writing? Are you ashamed of it? Don't be – be proud. Although yes, there may be ample justification for the writers of erotica to shelter behind a pen-name!

If you do decide that you need to adopt a pen-name there are virtually no problems. Write your short story, article or book and submit it as 'By Belinda Bloggs'.

At the foot of the cover page give your name and address as 'Joe Soap, writing as Belinda Bloggs'. Similarly, ensure that your notepaper heading is in your own name but also lists/mentions your pen-name(s). Editors and publishers will be accustomed to this process. If by chance a cheque arrives, payable to your pen-name – send it back, asking for it to be re-issued. Don't worry, the cheque will come back, but there may be some delay.

If, for some reason, you wish still further to preserve the secret of your pen-name, it is possible to open a separate bank account as 'Joe Soap, trading as Belinda Bloggs' – but this shouldn't be necessary.

I recommend that you establish yourself as a writer under your own name before you consider whether or not you need a pen-name.

### Is there a professional association – a 'trade union' – for writers?

There are several relevant organisations. If your writing activities are largely in the book-writing field – fiction or non-fiction – then the best is the Society of Authors. If your writing is more associated with radio, TV or stage, then your first choice would be The Writers' Guild of Great Britain. If you are primarily a journalist, then the National Union of Journalists (NUJ), which has a freelance section, would be most appropriate.

All three of those organisations will offer members assistance in areas of writing other than their major interest. (I am a member of the Society of Authors and they have helped me in extracting overdue payments for articles.)

Contact these organisations as below:

**Society of Authors**, 84 Drayton Gardens, London SW10 9SB. Tel: 020 7373 6642. Fax: 020 7373 5768. E-mail: authorsoc@writers.org.uk

Membership is open to authors who have had a full-length work published, broadcast or performed commercially in the UK. Associate membership is open to authors who have had a full-length work accepted for publication, but not yet published.

Membership subscription is basically £75, with various 'adjustments' available.

**The Writers' Guild of Great Britain**, 430 Edgware Road, London W2 1EH. Tel: 020 7723 8074. Fax: 020 7706 2413. E-mail: postie@wggb.demon.co.uk

> Membership is open to all persons entitled to claim a single piece of written work of any length for which payment has been received under written contract in terms not less favourable than those existing in current minimum terms agreements negotiated by the Guild.
>
> Membership subscription is £100 plus 1 per cent of that part of a writer's income earned from professional writing sources in the previous calendar year.

**National Union of Journalists**, Acorn House, 314-320 Gray's Inn Road, London WC1X 8DP. Tel: 020 7278 7916. Fax: 020 7837 8143. E-mail: nuj@mcr1.pop-tel.org.uk

> Membership is open to working journalists earning a significant income from writing.

### Why should I join a (writers') trade union – do I have to? And what's in it for me?

A writer's life is inevitably a solitary one. Alone, most writers cannot hope to stand up against the strength – the clout – of editors and publishers. By banding together, though, writers can negotiate for improvements in their lot. And they have done so, with considerable success.

The Society of Authors and The Writers' Guild together, fought long, hard and successfully for the introduction of Public Lending Right whereby authors earn a small fee for every borrowing of their books from Britain's public libraries. (*See* Chapter 4.) And the two bodies regularly campaign/negotiate for increases in the PLR funding.

The two bodies have also worked together to obtain publishers' agreement to minimum contractual terms for authors. Variations of the Minimum Terms Agreement have been accepted by a number of major publishers – even publishers who have not formally agreed the terms have moved towards them.

The Guild regularly negotiates with the BBC and commercial TV companies for improved fee for radio and TV scripts. And, more generally, all the writers' unions provide legal and other assistance to their members. The Society will vet an Agreement offered to an author – which can be an invaluable service to a first-time author particularly.

All three organisations publish their own magazines which keep members up-to-date on the writing world.

Do you HAVE to join one of these organisations? No. There is no compulsion whatsoever. Non-member book-writers will still gain all the benefits negotiated or fought for by the Society and the Guild – but not the advice and support available to members. Membership of the NUJ may bring higher rates of payment for magazine-writers.

There is strength in collective membership.

# 3

# JOINING UP THE WORDS

**How can I develop a 'good' writing style?**

Your writing style is very much your own. There are few hard and fast rules. And as you progress, and become increasingly confident in your writing skills, you can begin to break the 'rules'. The only requirement is that your writing should be understandable. And I believe too, that it should be an 'easy read'. I don't want anyone to have to work to understand my words.

The 'rules' then:

- Keep your writing clear and simple. Short words and short sentences are easier to understand than longer ones. So, for fiction and non-fiction alike:

a) prefer short, simple words to long, 'difficult-to-understand' ones. Not all readers have a dictionary immediately to hand – if they don't understand a word you are in danger of losing them.

b) prefer short sentences to long ones. At least until you are more experienced, I recommend an average sentence length of 15 words and a maximum length of 25 words. But vary your sentence lengths – too many short sentences will 'feel' jumpy; too many roughly-15-word sentences will be boring; too many long sentences will be soporific.

- Long paragraphs *look* hard to understand, so keep them short. I suggest an average of maybe 60 words per paragraph and a maximum of 120 (for magazines) to 150 (for books). The off-putting appearance of a long paragraph is partly related to the column width – 100 words in a wide column might look easy to read; the same wordage in a narrow newspaper column will look long and difficult. And remember: only one topic per paragraph – a fresh topic warrants a fresh para.

- Link paragraphs together – by the opening words of each new para referring back to the content of its predecessor – to improve the overall 'flow' of the writing. (Real 'joined up' writing.)

- Avoid a second use of the same word (other than 'the', 'and', etc.) within the same or adjacent sentences: think of a different way of saying the same thing. And watch out for your own 'favourite' words and expressions. Don't use them.

- Avoid – and this is a pet hate of my own – most uses of the word 'very'. It is seldom necessary.

- Avoid pompous-sounding expressions. We all write them in the first draft. The successful writer recognises them – and deletes or rewrites them. The best way of identifying them is to read your work aloud.

## How many drafts should I produce before I consider my novel/story/book/article complete?

Each writer must make their own judgement/decision on this. You must go through as many drafts as necessary to satisfy yourself that the result is the best you can do. The competition for publication is so fierce that *only* your best will do – and even that may not be good enough.

Every time you send anything to an editor or publisher you are entering the most important writing competition of all; you are competing with your peers for publication. Each acceptance means you're a winner. If the work you submit is not your best, you don't stand a chance of winning. And it is only by re-drafting and polishing your work that you will achieve your best. So take as many drafts as you need.

Some writers prefer not to do too much re-drafting and polishing, claiming that there is a danger of losing the *freshness* of the original thoughts. Others will spend ages searching for the *exact* word … and produce so little finished work that no one notices them. You must make your own decision as to how much re-drafting and polishing you do. I firmly believe that EVERYONE'S work can be improved by a certain amount of polishing, changing a word here, deleting one there, without necessarily exposing oneself to the trauma of major re-drafting.

Working direct onto a word processor, as I now do, I struggle to express my thoughts and ideas as simply and understandably as possible in my initial draft. Every now and then – at least once a day – while the draft is still only on the computer file, I re-read on the screen what I have written so far. At this read-through I can spot many of the faults – closely adjacent re-use of the same word, for instance – and sort them out.

When writing to a tight length constraint, such as for an article, I will also, at this stage, cut any excess wordage, all the time watching the word count. The result is always more taut and reads better.

When the chapter or article is complete, I print out a hard copy. I read these pages very carefully – it always seems different than when it's merely on the screen – and make further corrections. Sometimes I read a tricky section aloud, to convince myself that it is as well phrased, and as easy a read, as I can manage. And that's usually it. I save the corrections and print out the final version – preferably the next day, when it gets a final quick read-through.

## How long should my article/story/non-fiction book/novel be?

As long as it needs to be, but within any constraints imposed by the specific market.

If you are writing an article or short story for a magazine you will know – either from editorial guidelines or from your own research – how long it should be. If you submit a 2,000-word article or short story to a magazine which only takes one-page articles or stories of around 800 to 1,000 words, it will be rejected. You can bank on that. If a magazine wants 800–1,000 words they want 800–1,000 words – not 'as long as it needs to be'. Your words are there to fill the space around the income-producing advertisements.

The constraints on book-writing are less onerous. BUT – your proposed book has to be book length. Many publishers believe that the public buys books by weight. Documents of five to ten thousand words do not make a book. (Except perhaps for younger children.) At the other extreme, you would find it hard to persuade a publisher to accept a book which was 200,000 words long. (Too heavy to read in bed.)

Romance novels are usually written to a specific length laid down by the publisher. Some novels within the Harlequin Mills & Boon list are restricted to about 55,000 words, as they are required to fit into a standard 192-page book. Most other genre novels are at least 70,000 words long and not many exceed 120,000 words.

You will seldom go far wrong if your first novel runs out at about 100,000 words.

Few adult non-fiction books would be less than, say, 20,000 words long – and at that length would need to be one of a series, and written to strict format and 'organisational' requirements. A how-to book such as this one will usually be around 40,000 words long. A travel book or biography would seldom be less than 50,000 words long, and most would be perhaps 70,000 plus. An upper limit – at least for first thoughts – would once again probably be 100,000 words.

## Will too much polishing destroy the spontaneity of my work?

By definition, too much polishing will be too much. The right amount though, is beneficial – and almost always necessary.

Until you gain confidence in your writing skills, it is a good idea to retain an unaltered copy of your first draft, so that you can compare your later version with the original. You can then judge whether all of your polishing has been beneficial or whether, for the sake of spontaneity, you might prefer to go back to some parts of the original version.

Particularly in article writing, the polishing process will often involve cutting – getting rid of the waffle, the unintended pomposities, and the repetitions – getting down to length. To actually provide for such cutting, it is worth writing your article a bit over length – say, ten per cent. A ten per cent cut then not only trims to length, but also tightens up the writing beneficially.

When writing fiction, you should be particularly careful with the dialogue. We don't always 'talk proper'; there is a real danger of losing the naturalness of dialogue by over-polishing.

**From where should I get the characters for my stories?**

Some writers base their characters on real people. Other writers put together an amalgam of relevant parts of a number of 'real' people. Others get their characters direct from their imagination. Indeed, because we can seldom really know *everything* about a real person, even if a fictional character is initially based on just one acquaintance, the author will always have to use his/her imagination to further develop the character within the story.

Some writers collect newspaper and magazine photographs of 'interesting-looking' people. This helps them to invent their next character. They bestow on the pictured character as many unattributable characteristics as necessary.

What it boils down to, therefore, is that, irrespective of their 'starting point' your characters come from your imagination. There will be a bit of you in every one of your fictional characters.

Whatever the initial source of your fictional characters it is useful to write a potted biography of each before you start on their story. You need to know your characters well: to understand what makes them tick, to know how they will react in the various situations you put them in.

Make a list of personal characteristics – looks, likes and dislikes, birth date, social background, political leanings, etc. – and fill in the details. Dick Winfield, in his excellent *One Way to Write Your Novel* (Writer's Digest, Cincinatti, 1969) suggests developing a series of two-answer questions – beautiful or ugly, well-dressed or scruffy, generous or mean – and determining the character's personality by ... tossing a coin. The more detailed – and inconsequential – the questions, the more the character will come alive. It's worth a try.

Jean Saunders' book, *How to Create Fictional Characters* (Allison & Busby, London, 1992) contains much good, practical advice on character creation and development.


**What do I do if people recognise themselves in my stories?**

You should have thought about that before you used them so obviously.

To avoid such a situation, refer back to the previous answer – an amalgam of several people seasoned with a generous helping of your own imagination will seldom create such a problem. But again, as above, even the character based on just one real person will inevitably have some characteristics that are *not* identifiable – and you can perhaps cite those in your 'defence'.


**How much dialogue, how much description, and how much action should there be in a novel?**

There cannot be a definitive answer to such a question. Books are not written to rule. And different types, different *genres* will have different proportions.

But various pundits have offered fairly consistent advice.

Perhaps the most positive advice comes from Dianne Doubtfire – who has inspired many aspiring novelists – in her *Creative Writing*. She suggest that the breakdown should be 'one third dialogue, one third action and one third introspection.' But she also stresses that this will vary with the type of fiction.

Top novelist John Braine, in his *Writing a Novel*, suggests as a working rule that 'not more than one-half of any novel should be dialogue'. And he warns that every line of dialogue should advance the story.

Dorothea Brande however, commenting on the use of dialogue, in *Becoming a Writer* suggests that writers need to decide whether they want to write fiction or to specialise in playwriting. Ouch!

But anyway, as Alice questioned, 'What is the use of a book without … conversations?'

Clearly, there is no rule, but Dianne Doubtfire's advice seems about right, depending on circumstances and the need of *your* novel.


**How should I differentiate, in the text, between speech and thoughts?**

It is customary to show speech (dialogue) within single quote marks. (But some publishers – a declining bunch – have a house style requiring the use of double quotes for speech. They will tell you – or make the changes for you.) One way to indicate a character's thoughts is then to show them in italics – indicated in your typescript by underlining. I would favour this method if there's going to be a lot to it.

Another way of indicating thoughts is to omit the quote marks, but introduce the thought with a capital letter. Thus:

And then, she thought, This won't do at all, my girl.

Or, of course, to show the thought indirectly:

This wouldn't do at all, she thought.

As always, the answer is probably to ring the changes.

### How do I polish my first draft?

The term 'polishing' implies a general tidying up and improvement of your work. Some suggestions for possible improvements:

- Cut out the waffle – the words and phrases that are not necessary to move the story or description forward.
- Cut out the qualifications of the unqualifiable – the 'slightly pregnants', the 'very uniques'.
- Cut out the obvious, such as: 'Clearly …' (If it's clear, you needn't say so.); 'And, of course, …'; and obviously, 'Obviously, …'
- Cut out the repetitions – of thoughts, words and phrases.
- Consider subdividing and/or re-writing over-long sentences – those in excess of 25 words. Similarly, consider sub-dividing longer paragraphs.
- Check the punctuation – particularly for an excess of commas – and, except perhaps within dialogue, delete just about every exclamation mark. An explanation mark usually suggests a less-than-competent writer.
- Make sure that you have only used underlining in your typescript where you

need the underlined words to be shown in italics. It is not a good way of showing emphasis.
• Make sure that, throughout, your meaning will be clear to the reader.


## How may I avoid the over-use of 'he/she said'?

To a large extent, the words 'he/she said' become invisible. Readers tend to ignore them. You can worry too much about their use. There are two or three ways of getting around the need for attribution without excessive repetition of the dreaded words. You can:

• use just 'he/she said', but less often – just enough to avoid the reader losing track of who is speaking.
• use some of the many synonyms – muttered, whispered, shouted, etc. – when appropriate.
• use the other person's name when addressing them, thereby making clear who is speaking.

Use a variety of the above methods. But, above all, remember that the reader wants to get on with the story. The sole purpose of the attributions is to aid that process.

The methods are best illustrated by a couple of examples, both using the same, 'hammy' dialogue. First, how not to do it – the over-use of 'he/she said':

> 'Listen to me,' he said.
> 'Yes, dear, what is it?' she said.
> 'I wanted to tell you that I love you,' he said.
> 'How nice,' she said.
> 'Is that all you can say?' he said.
> 'I thought that words were no longer necessary,' she said.

Compare that with this version, using a variety of methods, which despite the still 'hammy' dialogue, is undoubtedly much better:

'Listen to me, Mabel.'

'Yes, dear, what is it?'

'I wanted to tell you that I love you.' His arms tightened lovingly around her.

'Ummm, nice.'

'Is that all – ouch – you can say?'

'I thought,' she said, and her voice was muffled as she gently nibbled his ear, 'that words …' She paused again, to kiss more thoroughly, 'were no longer necessary.' She disentangled a hand, reached behind her, and switched off the light.

**My friends tell me that my writing is good, yet I seem to get nothing but rejections. Is this unusual?**

Not at all. Every writer gets, or has had, rejections. There are many tales of now-famous writers who once papered their walls with rejection slips. Such tales are almost certainly apocryphal but I went to a lecture once where the speaker, a writer, had a really huge display board covered with rejection slips – as a visual aid. It made quite an impression.

When you start writing, you are learning the trade or craft. And the best way to learn is to do. It is not an inborn natural instinct to write the way editors want. You have to learn how to join words together in the most effective way: to write crisply. And that takes time.

You think your work is fit for publishing: the best way to find out if you're right is to submit it to an editor. An editor is the most important arbiter of writing ability: the editor is the one person who says yea or nay. Anyone else's judgement – particularly friends' – is irrelevant.

The most important thing is not to let the inevitable rejections cause you to lose heart. A writer needs to be resilient.

And remember: a rejection slip can come for a variety of reasons outside of your control:

• The magazine may already have used – or have in the immediate pipeline – a similar article or short story. The editor will not wish to duplicate it.
• The magazine may have an unwritten policy not to feature some aspect of

your article or short story. (The editor of one well-known women's magazine will not allow story characters to smoke.)

- The magazine may have an over-large stock of material and is therefore rejecting everything. Or maybe the magazine is suffering a cash flow crisis – in which case rejection may be a good thing. Publication without being paid is a worst-case scenario – you can no longer offer F.B.S.R. elsewhere – *see* Chapter 5.

Other – more likely – reasons for rejection are discussed in response to the next question.

**What, and how, can I learn from my rejections?**

I suppose that, if we all followed all of the advice and instruction available on how to write, market and present our work we would, apart from the unforeseeable reasons above, never get a rejection slip. But we are all human. Most of us will, at least sometimes, write something and, in a fit of enthusiasm, immediately send it off to a magazine we've just heard about. That way usually means rejection.

So, let's see what we can interpret from a rejected piece of work:

- Did you submit it to an appropriate magazine? Not all magazines will accept unsolicited material; some will only accept fiction, some only feature articles. You need to be aware of these matters, and much more – *see* next chapter.
- Were the length and style right for the particular market? Indeed, if an article, did you write it specifically to the magazine's requirements? An over-long article or story, no matter how good in itself, will never sell to a magazine which has a limit on lengths. And a magazine's preferred style is often specific.
- Did your article or short story really *grab* the reader within the first few lines? If it didn't have a good *hook*, the editor won't have bothered to read any more. The opening paragraph is perhaps the most important part of any article or short story. You must work hard on your opening. You may have to rewrite it several times to get it right. The title too is important, although

maybe less so. Aim for a short, punchy title. But be prepared for the editor to re-title it: every editor believes his/her titles are best.

- In your article, were you saying something worth saying? Was the article packed with useful/interesting facts – put across in an interesting, even entertaining, way? Did you incorporate some relevant anecdotes and/or quotes? Simply rehashing tired old ideas and well-known facts in a tired old way won't work.

- In your story, was there a fresh twist to the plot and were the characters alive? OK, so there are only supposed to be so many basic plots – your job is to make yours different. You **DO NOT** want the editor to guess the end right at the start.

- Was your article or short story *right* for its length? One episode, one anecdote, won't make a story; you can't compress a book-length (non-fiction) subject into a single feature. Did you have sufficient factual information to fill the article – without padding.

- Was the sequence, the framework, of the short story or article clear and readily understood by the reader?

- Was your story made confusing by an excess of bit-part characters – with insufficiently disparate names? Avoid having Bob, Bert, Betty and Barbara all in the same story. And have no more than a small handful of essential participants.

- Did your work, as submitted, *look good*? A busy editor will often pass by an untidy-looking, messy submission in favour of a well-presented one. (*See* Chapter 9.)

And to avoid getting dispirited, once you've worked through that checklist, always remember that there may have been some other reason for your rejection. See the previous question.

**Do experienced and successful writers still get rejections?**

Oh, yes. If only it were not so. Hopefully though, the rejections just get fewer as the writers become more experienced.

As mentioned elsewhere (chapter 8), there is a growing tendency for editors to give at least tentative decisions about feature articles on the basis of preliminary outlines/queries. At least, when an outline is rejected, the follow-up article, which might equally have been rejected, doesn't get written.

A short story is nearly always a speculative piece of work. Not everyone will enjoy it. There are bound to be occasional rejections.

With novels, the experienced author will usually submit a synopsis plus the first three chapters: this will result in either acceptance, or rejection or suggestions for amendment to ensure acceptance.

And with non-fiction books, while most of the book will not be written before it is commissioned, many ideas will have fallen by the wayside earlier.

All of that said, I still get my share of rejections – of article ideas, of non-fiction book ideas, and of adventure book story-lines. But when I'm actually joining words together, as opposed to formulating and submitting ideas, I am usually fairly assured of forthcoming acceptance.

Guessing, I would say that if all of my rejected non-fiction book ideas had been accepted, I'd have written and published getting on for twice as many books. But they wouldn't necessarily have sold well. Publishers tend to know what will sell and what won't.

Successful writers are the ones who learn from their rejections.

# 4

# WHO FOR - AND FOR HOW MUCH?

**Why do I need to do market research?**

It's easiest to understand the need for market research if you consider the extremes. A short story intended for the children's page in, say, *People's Friend,* would obviously be very different from a science fiction short story aimed at *interzone.* An article aimed at *Country Life* would need to be written in a different way from one, even on the same subject, written for *The Lady.*

Different magazines have different readerships and material written for one needs to be written differently for another. Unless the writer knows the particular requirements of a specific 'target' magazine, a submission will probably not be accepted.

The concept of market research is so obvious that it is hard to understand why so much material is submitted by beginners to inappropriate magazines. Yet this is certainly the case: editors regularly complain about writers not having reviewed their magazine before submitting work.

Market research is not just a matter of writing 'in the right way' for a specific magazine. Different magazines will have different requirements in terms of:

- overall length: many magazines organise their content to be complete within single or double pages – without follow-ons. Thus, an 1,100-word short story may not fit into a one-page 'slot'. And different magazines have different page wordages.
- sentence and paragraph length: long sentences can be difficult to understand; long paragraphs tend to *look* difficult ('heavy'). A 100-word paragraph in a half-page-width column will occupy less column space, and therefore *look* shorter – and less 'heavy' – than the same para in a narrow, newspaper column. Different magazines use different column widths.

- feature and short story subjects: magazines vary widely in the subjects they will handle – some are uninhibited, even raunchy; others are very 'old-fashioned'.
- number and ages of characters in short stories: the shorter the short story, the fewer the characters it can carry; and readers like to identify with main characters – who should therefore be of similar age to the readers. The target readers of different magazines vary in their ages.
- number, provision and type of illustrations: some magazines will use only one or two illustrations per feature article, others many more; some still use mainly black-and-white, other mostly colour; some magazines use a lot of specialist illustrators, others welcome 'words-and-pix' package submissions (to identify, compare the photographic credits with the writer's byline).
- overall treatment: depending on their readership different magazines will treat similar subjects in different ways – one magazine will be brash and 'tabloidy' in its treatment; another staid and 'broadsheety'.

Unless a writer studies his/her target magazines the likelihood of success is considerably reduced.

Book publishers too need evidence of market research by writers. More of this below, but once again, considering extremes, Harlequin Mills & Boon will consider romance fiction (of carefully specified length) – but no non-fiction; How To Books will consider carefully targeted non-fiction books – but no romances.

Market research is an essential part of the writer's job.

**Is there any market research information readily available to magazine writers?**

Yes. But remember that published information can never be as useful as a writer's own research. And, inevitably, in the fast-changing world of magazine-publishing, printed information – which takes time to get from contact advice or market study to new writer's desk-top – is quickly out of date.

There are three basic sources of published market research information:

- the annual (or biennial) writers' handbooks
- writers' magazines
- magazines' own writers'/contributors' guidelines

First, the handbooks. Again, there are three in the UK:

*The Writers' & Artists' Yearbook* (with a red cover), published annually by A. & C. Black – this contains summarised information on about 800 U.K. and Irish magazines and a hundred-plus national and regional newspapers and 200-plus newspapers and magazines in other English-speaking countries. It also contains information about book publishers – see below.

*The Writers' Handbook* (with a yellow cover), published annually by Macmillan – much the same sort of information as in the *Writers' & Artists'* but presented in a somewhat more informal – and anecdotally informative – way.

*The Magazine Writer's Handbook* currently prepared by Chriss McCallum and myself – originally in the Allison & Busby Writers' Guides series but now published approximately biennially by Writers' Bookshop. The book is aimed purely and simply at writers like us. It contains a full page of detailed market information about each of 70-odd carefully selected 'mainstream' magazines of particular interest to the 'ordinary' freelance – including just what sort of features and short stories they have used in the recent past, the target readership and how best to approach the editor – plus more condensed information about several dozen smaller 'independent press' magazines.

(In the US, the equivalent of the *Writers' & Artists'* is, of course, the annual *Writer's Market*, obtainable from Writer's Digest (Books) at the address on page 14.)

A typical magazine entry in the *Writers' & Artists'* would be something like this:

**The Widget Collector**
Widget House, 76 Muddlecombe Road,
Muddling-on-Mullet, Borsetshire MU9 &XX
*tel* 01234 567890 *fax* 01234 567891
*e-mail* kevin@widget.co.uk

*website* http://www.widget.co.uk
*editor* Kevin Widgeter
Monthly £3.75

Technical and semi-technical articles, 500–5,000 words, on design, history, and use of standard and one-off widgets. Short stories if relating to widgets.

Payment: by arrangement. Illustrations welcomed: line, half-tone, colour. Founded 1923.

Clearly, while such entries give a brief overview of each magazine listed, they leave much for the freelance writer to find out for him/herself. Within that very wide wordage range, what length is actually preferred? Short stories about widgets? Really? And what sort of length? Payment by arrangement could be anything from £10 to £150, per thousand words. Colour prints or slides? The writer would need to do a lot more market research work before submitting material to this magazine.

Next, the writing magazines. The main British and American magazines have already been listed – *see* page 14. There are also, however, two independent, smaller-circulation market research magazines-cum-newsletters in Britain, both very good, both purely market- (and writers-competition-) oriented:

*Freelance Market News*, 11 issues per year, each of 16 A4 pages, by subscription only, £29 p.a., from Sevendale House, 7 Dale Street, Manchester M1 1JB.
*Writers' Bulletin*, 6 issues per year, each of 28 A5 pages, by post, £2 per issue post free, from Cherrybite Publications, Linden Cottage, 45 Burton Road, Little Neston, Cheshire CH64 4AE.

And, thirdly, the writer can approach 'target magazines' directly, asking for Contributors' Guidelines, if any are available. American magazines have long provided such guidelines; starting from an almost non-existent base, U.K. magazines are increasingly making them available – often, also, on the Internet. They are always extremely valuable – but still need to be checked, personally, against an *up-to-date* issue of the relevant magazine. Six-month-old issues flipped through in the dentist's waiting room are no substitute for proper market study – see below.

# WHO FOR – AND FOR HOW MUCH?

## How do I do a writer's market research appraisal of a magazine?

Initially, select just two or three varied magazines which you are going to target: you can't expect, at least not straight away, to know all about lots of different magazines. It's wise to choose magazines that are not directly in competition with each other.

Concentrate on only a few at first. I would go for one general interest (probably women's) magazine, one on your personal specialism and one countryside magazine (your local county magazine maybe) or one of the national 'nostalgia' mags such as *Best of Britain* or *This England*. Next, and again, this cannot be over-emphasised, you need two or three *up-to-date* issues of the magazine.

First, flip through the pages of one of the magazines to get an overall 'feel' for it. Is it brash or sedate, colourful or rather dull-looking? Are the feature headlines apparently (or really) uninhibited; do the short story titles suggest somewhat raunchy tales?

Next, look carefully at the advertisements. These will give you a good idea of the typical reader. Retirement homes and stair lifts suggest a 'mature-plus' readership; children's clothes and toys suggest a readership of young mums; child-friendly breakfast cereals also suggest a young mum, with growing family; adverts for half-million pound homes and top-of-the-market cars or perfume, suggest an affluent readership; cheap mail-order clothes, the reverse.

Reinforce your growing feel for the typical reader by looking at the Letters and 'agony' pages, if there are any. From these pages you can usually get a clear idea of the readers' ages and their life-style. Read the short stories: what age are the main characters? The readers are about the same age as the characters – readers like to identify themselves with the characters.

Check your idea of the typical reader by repeating the same appraisal of the other sample issues of the same magazine. And it's wise then to write down a pen picture of the reader – memory is ever fallible.

Now go to the Contents page – and it will help to have all the samples open there at the same time. Identify the regular features and columns. If nothing else, the same byline appearing through your three issues will probably mean a regular or staff writer. You would be well-advised to avoid writing features that overlap/clash with regular columns: if the editor is committed to paying the regular writer, he probably won't want submissions on the regulars' subjects from elsewhere.

Look at the sort of feature that, by its byline, appears to have been supplied by an 'ordinary' writer like you and I. Any features written by a household name can be crossed off your list: you can't compete – they were commissioned. Somewhere on the Contents page (or elsewhere, on a 'masthead' page) you may find a list of editorial staff. It's worth checking the staff names against the contributors' by-lines – and avoiding competing with the staff. The staff will almost always win.

In most magazines there will still be a few features left that might have been written by someone like you, had you thought of it, and got there in time. These are the ones on which you need to model your early submissions.

Check the subjects, the overall length, the average paragraph and sentence lengths, the *way* the article was put together. Check too for long – and therefore 'difficult' – words; few casual magazine readers have dictionaries readily to hand.

Move on now to the stories. There may be one short-short (around a thousand words – usually complete on a single page) and one or two longer short stories. Again – but this time with more care and attention – check the ages of the main characters, the type of story (genre, twist-in-tail, etc.) and, again, most important, the length. Do the love scenes stop at the bedroom door, or go on in? Are the short stories mostly by well-known names? 'Names' are hard to compete with. How much dialogue is there in the story? Is the story told in first, or third person – and whose? And check the *exact* length of the short-short story – a hundred words over or under could mean rejection of what might otherwise be a sure-fire success.

Like the pen-picture of the typical reader, it will pay you to make notes of your market research studies. But you need to up-date them frequently – editorial staff are always moving about and old ideas often go with them.

Having identified typical feature articles and/or short stories you now KNOW exactly what the editor liked and accepted – back then. If your research is fairly current, this is probably what the editor will STILL want. Except that he/she wants something different. Your job is to produce something with the pulling power of your model, on a not-too-different subject or theme, treated in much the same way – but FRESH and NEW.

**What about market research for book writers? What do I need to do and how do I do it?**

As mentioned above, book publishers are all different; a book unattractive and boring to one, might easily be just what another is desperately looking for. It is the author's job to find the 'right' publisher for his/her new book. (You have to kiss an awful lot of 'froggy-publishers' before you find a princely one.) One small plus point though – publishers' policies and requirements don't usually change as quickly as do those of magazine editors.

The first port of call for an unagented British author doing market research for his/her book will, in Britain, usually be the two yearbooks mentioned above:

The *Writers' & Artists' Yearbook* (A. & C. Black)
*The Writers' Handbook* (Macmillan)

Both give details of several hundred publishers. (Once again, American writers can consult the excellent annual *Writer's Market* – from Writer's Digest Books, address on page 14.)

A typical publisher entry in the *Writers' & Artists'* would be something like:

**Widget Publishers Ltd**
Widget House, 76 Muddlecombe Road,
Muddling-on-Mullet, Borsetshire MU9 &XX
*tel* 01234 567892 *fax* 01234 567893
*e-mail* kevin@widgetbooks.co.uk
*website* http://www.widgetbooks.co.uk
*Managing Editor* Kevin Widgeter

Highly illustrated technical books for adults. Children's illustrated fiction.and non-fiction.
Subsidiary of Widget Books Inc.
Founded 1983.

As with magazines, *The Writers' Handbook* is more forthcoming, with anecdotal quotes, etc. Even if expanded in that way though, it is clear that the publisher-seeking author needs to know more than is available in these yearbooks.

Another book listing British book publishers – and including many of the smaller, independent publishers excluded from the two major yearbooks – is:

*The Guide to Book Publishers*, annually, from Writers' Bookshop

But the author still needs more.

The next step is to consult one of the six-monthly bumper issues of the U.K. book trade weekly magazine *The Bookseller*. This is expensive to buy but most public libraries will have a copy available; if it's not on the shelves, ask the librarian. The inch-thick Spring and Autumn *Buyers Guides* issues list most of the new books to be published by most publishers within the following half-year. Novels are listed by type/genre and by author; non-fiction books are listed by subject area and publisher.

As well as the categorised editorial listing, half of each bumper issue consists of publishers' advertisements. These too give a good indication of the types of books each publisher is interested in.

From the brief listings in the yearbooks and the subject-area listings and adverts in *The Bookseller*, the author will be able to identify a handful of possibly appropriate publishers for his/her forthcoming book. The handful will sometimes be large, sometimes small: larger is better. At this stage it is worth phoning each of the 'selected' publishers and asking (usually the telephone operator) for a copy of the publishers' latest catalogue. You will usually be successful – which saves you the cost of sending a stamped addressed envelope for the catalogue.

You will be able to get some idea, from the catalogues mainly, but also from the *Bookseller* listings, of the lengths of the books published by your chosen handful. You may find lengths quoted by numbers of book pages: as a first rough guide, assume 400 words per book page.

If yours is a non-fiction book, look specifically for series into which your book could be adjusted to fit. Series are good because new books tend to sell best on the backs of their predecessors.

Check the catalogue-content against your potential bestseller. Does this publisher look likely to be interested in your book? Do they publish similar titles?

At this stage, you MUST now have a look at one or two books, similar to yours, from the publishers of your choice. Yours needs to be *somewhat* along the same lines – length, genre, etc. – but, as for magazines, FRESH and NEW.

All that checking done, trust your judgement and submit your synopsis and/or sample chapters – and good luck.

## How much am I likely to earn from my writing – that is, how much per story, article or book?

Inevitably, this is very much a 'How long is a piece of string?' type question. The answers depend very much on the market to which you are selling your work.

Initially, forget the 'book' part of the question. Short stories and articles sell to magazines. There are 'mainstream' magazines – those on the shelves of newsagents – and there are 'independent' or 'small press' magazines – small circulation publications, produced by dedicated individuals or groups, and usually sold only on subscription.

Short stories and/or articles sold to the independent magazines do not attract large payments. Some pay nothing at all, merely a few copies of the magazine in which the work appears. Those small press magazines that do pay, seldom pay more than maybe £20 per piece..

But most writers expect (or hope) to sell their work to the mainstream magazines. Pay rates in this sector vary widely. Articles are usually paid at so much per thousand words and the mainstream rate can be as low as maybe £30-40 per thousand – or well over £100. An average of maybe £60-70 per thousand words would not be an unreasonable assumption.

Short stories for the mainstream magazines – which are largely targeted at women readers – are usually paid for at so much per story. The tightly-written thousand-word 'short-short' or 'coffee-break' story can entail as much writing effort as a more relaxed 2,500-worder. Few mainstream magazines will pay less than £100 for a story – some, pay several hundred pounds.

It is worth remembering that the competition for articles and short stories will often be less at the magazines that pay below average rates; the lower-paying markets therefore, are good places to learn the trade – to 'serve your apprenticeship'. Michelangelo undoubtedly did a lot of less prestigious and less well paid work before he was commissioned to decorate the ceiling of the Sistine Chapel.

Now, books – about which it is easier to answer.

Most books, both fiction and non-fiction, are paid for in 'royalties' (see Chapter 7, page 92). As already indicated, hardback royalties are usually around 10 per cent and paperback royalties around 7.5 per cent. Not many hardback books – and seldom those by 'first-time authors' – sell more than, say, 1,500 copies; at a list price of, say, £16 the total earnings would therefore be

$$1,500 \times 0.1 \times £16 = £2,400$$

against which has to be set, an advance of maybe £1,500 (based on the earnings from half the print run.

Similarly, a trade paperback on 7.5 per cent royalties on a list price of £10, might sell virtually all of a 3,000 copy print run. This would generate

$$3,000 \times 0.075 \times £10 = £2,250$$

of which, about half would already have been paid as an advance.

Overall, reckon on earning no more than about £2,000 for a first book – and that, spread over time. If the book is really successful, though, and sales take off, if it is re-issued as a mass market paperback, then the earnings – particularly for a novel – can increase spectacularly and unpredictably. (But equally, lots of books never 'earn out' their advance.)

Writing – whether short pieces for magazines or full-length books – is no easy road to riches. If you could write (and sell) one short story or article per week at, say, £150 per time, your total annual earnings would amount to no more than £7,500. Similarly, if you could write (and sell) a new book every three months, earning £2,000 for each, your annual earnings would be just £8,000. Even if you doubled the output, or the payments, the resultant £15-16,000 is not riches. And few of us are lucky enough – or skilled enough – to sell everything we write.

Advice: don't give up the day job.

## Do well-known writers get paid more than others?

Of course. If you saw an announcement on the cover of one magazine that there was a short story inside, by your favourite big-name writer, and on another, similar magazine that there was a story inside by Belinda Bloggs, which magazine would you buy? The big name attracts more readers – and the story is therefore of greater 'pulling value' to the magazine publisher.

The same principle would apply to an opinion-type article. Readers are likely to be more interested in the opinions of a major politician or TV personality than in the views of someone they've never heard of. So the 'name' will probably be paid more than the 'nobody'.

If a well-known person writes a first non-fiction book, their name will help to sell the book; the publisher will expect larger sales and will almost certainly offer a larger than usual advance against royalties. The royalty rate however will probably be 'the standard'. Similarly, a well-known author can negotiate better terms than a first-timer for a new novel.

## What is PLR?

The initials PLR stand for Public Lending Right. Under the terms of the Public Lending Right Act of 1979, payment is made from central government funds, to authors whose books are borrowed from public libraries. Illustrators, editors and translators too, if mentioned on the book's title page, are eligible for a share in a book's PLR. An *Information for Authors* leaflet is available from the PLR office.

The existence of the PLR Act owes much to the campaigning, over a number of years, by the Society of Authors and the Writers' Guild of Great Britain (see Chapter 2, page 26-7) and, in particular, by several well-known writers – notably Maureen Duffy and the late Brigid Brophy.

In 1999, The Registrar of Public Lending Right published a collection of essays, *Whose Loan is it Anyway?*, giving many insights into the struggle to establish PLR.

Details of book loans are collected annually from a broad sample of public library authorities. This data is then factored up, on a regional basis to arrive at a regional loans estimate for each PLR-registered book. The regional figures are then added together to give a national estimate for the loans of every book. PLR-registered authors are then paid a small amount in respect of each (estimated) loan.

The payment rate per loan varies each year depending on the amount of money made available by government, less the administrative costs of the PLR Office, and the total number of loans of registered books. (The February 2000 payment rate per loan for the period 1 July 1998 to 30 June 1999 was 2.18 pence.)

A few more interesting/important points:

• only books registered before 30 June receive any payment in the following February.
• books can only be registered when they are published – and have an ISBN.
• separate registrations are required for separate editions of a book – e.g., hardback and paperback – where such editions have different ISBNs.
• just over 30,000 authors, with a total of nearly 305,000 books, were PLR-registered for the February 2000 payments.
• a total of just over £4.2 million was paid to authors in February 2000.

### How do I register for PLR?

PLR application forms and full details of the scheme can be obtained from The Registrar, PLR Office, Richard House, Sorbonne Close, Stockton-on-Tees TS17 6DA. (Note: this is a new address.)

At around the end of each year, PLR-registered authors receive a detailed statement of their PLR earnings. Payments are made directly to the author's bank account a month or so later.

### How much can I earn from PLR?

There's that piece of string again. But at least we know finite 'length' limits. There is a limit to how much an author can earn from PLR – no matter how many titles or how many loans, no author can (currently) be paid more than £6,000. This maximum threshold is applied to around 100 registered authors. Earnings of less that £5 are carried over to the next year.

As mentioned above, there were just over 30,000 registered authors at February 2000. In round thousands, of these, 13,000 authors earned no PLR at all. Of the 17,000 'earning' authors, 12,000 received less that £100 and only 1,700 earned more than £500. The remaining nearly 3,500 authors earned between £100 and £500 for the year.

So, you probably won't earn a lot from PLR – but it **is** 'extra' money.


**If I only sell the occasional article or short story, do I have to report this income to the Income Tax authorities?**

Yes.


**How can I – legally – minimise the tax liability on my writing earnings?**

You are entitled to charge legitimate expenses against your earnings. Once you start trying to break into the writing business therefore, you should keep careful note of all your expenses.

You can't claim for the initial purchase of your 'tools of your trade' (computer, reference books, etc.) but you can claim for their replacement. Under current regulations, you can set one quarter of the cost of replacement capital items (the new PC, for example) against your writing earnings. (And the following year, you can set one quarter of the remaining three-quarters of the capital cost against income. And so on.)

Keep a note of all your postage expenses – you'll be surprised how they mount up ... and they are tax-deductible.

Depending on your writing earnings – i.e., if your total annual income is only a hundred or so pounds, deduction claims in the thousands are unrealistic – you can claim expenses on: postage, telephone charges, research expenses, travel costs, stationery, membership fees for writing organisations.

When your writing income becomes a significant amount – and only you can decide what that means – it may be worth investing in a self-employed pension. The pension contributions will be tax-deductible and the pension itself will be most welcome in your 'twilight years'.

**What is a kill fee? How do I get one – do I have to ask for it?**

If an editor actually commissions you to write an article or short story for a magazine and then, when you've done it, decides for any reason not to use it, he/she is breaking his/her contract with you. You have done the work as required; you are entitled to recompense. The kill fee is compensation for the work being 'killed off'.

The editor's commission will sometimes be in the form of a written contract and this may include a cancellation clause specifying the amount of any compensation for non-use of commissioned work. It would be nice to think that the kill fee would be the same as the originally agreed payment for the work – often it will be less. If you have such a written contract it will probably specify how you should go about getting the kill fee.

Without a written contract, but for a firmly commissioned piece of work, it would be appropriate for you to ask the editor for a kill fee. You might be able to negotiate on the amount – 50 per cent would not be unusual.

A kill fee may also be appropriate where a piece of work is submitted *on spec*, firmly accepted – and then not used. Again, it would be appropriate to ask for such a fee. The success of your request will depend on the firmness – and proof – of the acceptance of the work. Editors are understandably cautious about the firmness of their acceptances; they use phrases like, 'held for possible use in a future issue'. This is a typical 'soft' acceptance and you might have difficulty extracting a kill fee against such a limited commitment. The prudent writer carefully preserves all relevant correspondence against such situations – and I usually confirm important telephone conversations back in writing to an editor.

**I have written a number of articles for a magazine; they were all accepted and have been published. They have paid me for the first few, but the magazine**

**has now ceased publication, without paying me for the remaining (published) articles. I have written and phoned the magazine's offices, to no avail. What should I do now?**

The first thing to do is formally to record the amount owing to you. If you have already submitted invoices for each of the published but unpaid articles, then I suggest you send a Statement of Account, listing the unpaid invoices in detail – invoice dates, publication dates, article titles and possibly even relevant magazine page-numbers. Address invoices and statement to the magazine and post it.

If the 'dead' magazine was a one-off publication – in other words, the publisher only had the one magazine – then it is likely that the publisher has gone into receivership. By sending a formal Statement of Account, your claim for payment will at least be treated on a par with all others to whom the publisher owes money.

When a one-off magazine dies, the main outstanding debts are likely to be far more serious than the amounts owed to a few contributors: the printers and the tax authorities will probably have far greater claims. In such a situation, you will probably not get paid at all. It has happened, just like that, to me – more than once – and I have received nothing. Write it off as experience and try not to let unpaid payments pile up: delay delivering your next article until an overdue account is paid.

But many magazines are one of several from the same publisher. If this is the case with your magazine, I would contact the accounts department of the parent publisher. You should be able to persuade them to meet the outstanding amounts due to you. Write to them – politely – with all the details and copies of the invoices and Statements. In the last resort, if I could get no satisfaction from the parent publisher's accounts department, I would ask any professional writers trade union of which I was a member, to intervene on my behalf. (The Society of Authors – see page 26 – have helped me in such situations in the past.)

**When – and how – do I submit an invoice to a magazine editor or to a publisher?**

Different magazines, different publishers have different systems. Some require invoices, some don't. You need to find out what each magazine and each publisher wishes. Ask them – they won't bite.

The only variation from the above advice would be in the situation described in the previous question. If a magazine or publisher was defaulting on contracted payments, I would always send them an invoice – whether they wanted it or not – and back this up with a regular monthly Statement of Account.

Whenever, and for whatever reason, you submit an invoice, it is essential that you retain a copy; you may need to be able to produce one.

How should you prepare an invoice?

All I do is use a sheet of headed notepaper. At the top, centred, I type INVOICE in bold capitals. Beneath that, as for a business letter, I type the date and the name and address of the firm I am billing. For emphasis, I then type INVOICE again, scroll down a few lines, then type 'To:'. A few more lines down and I itemise the work for which payment is due and at the right margin, the amount. Typical wording might be:

'On-delivery' part of agreed advance for [BOOK TITLE]
(Full manuscript delivered [date].) ......................................................... £000.00


or


Agreed payment for First British Serial Rights in illustrated
article [TITLE] published in [Magazine] dated [date]. ........................... £000.00


A few lines further down the page, I type, 'Total due' and repeat the amount. Towards the bottom of the page, centred, I also type '(No VAT registration.)' If you are VAT-registered, you will need to provide your registration number.

When submitting a required invoice to a magazine to which work has been submitted *on spec*, you may not know how much you are likely to be paid for the work, nor when it is to be used. This is not a problem – merely leave these details blank for the editor to complete.

# 5

# SAFEGUARDING RIGHTS - AND ADDING PICTURES

## What is copyright all about?

Copyright law is much the same throughout the European Union. What follows is a simplified description of copyright as applied in the U.K. American copyright law is different and is summarised at the end of this answer.

As soon as a writer records his/her original thoughts on paper – or any other appropriate medium such as, nowadays, a word processor file – they are copyright and, while working for him or her self, the copyright belongs to the writer. There is no requirement for the copyright in your work to be registered. If you write something during the course of ongoing – i.e., other than freelance – employment, the copyright in that work belongs to your employer.

Copyright means that no one else may publish – i.e., 'copy' – your recorded thoughts without your permission. Your *published* work remains 'in copyright' until 70 years after your death. If, ghoulishly, you are published posthumously, the copyright remains valid for 70 years after publication.

The copyright that a writer owns is *in the form* in which the thoughts are expressed; it is the originality of the *expression* that is relevant. There is no copyright in facts – only in the way in which they are presented or communicated. There is no copyright in ideas *or plots* – only in the way in which these are developed and used. There is no copyright in a title – it is too short.

Strictly speaking, any use of someone else's copyright material – e.g., a quotation – in one's own writing is an infringement of copyright. In practice, brief quotations of text or verse for comment or criticism are usually allowed 'on the nod'. The trouble is that there are various views on the meaning of 'brief'. I have always understood that 40–50 words, or three or four lines, was an acceptable limit but Michael Legat, in the *Writers' & Artists' Yearbook* suggests that up to 400 words is permissible – but strictly 'for criticism or review'. I would recommend playing safe and sticking nearer to the lower limit.

If you wish to quote more than the aforementioned brief amount of someone else's writing, you need to obtain permission – unless it is out of copyright. Write to the author, c/o the publisher of the book from which the quote is to come, and ask for permission. Depending on the size and importance of the quotation, permission may be freely granted – or you may have to pay a sizeable fee. Your own publisher may be prepared to reimburse the quotation fee – check first. Whether free or purchased, you should obtain and carefully file, a written statement of the permission to quote; your publisher will wish to see it.

Be particularly careful about quoting the words of a popular song. Even the briefest quotation may be challenged – and, let's face it, few of us quote pop song words 'for comment or criticism' – and a fee required. Even the briefest song extract quotation can mean payment of hundreds of pounds. The best advice is don't.

Whether a quotation of another writer's work is short or long, you should acknowledge who it is from. If someone was quoting from you, you'd want your name to be mentioned – so, do unto others … Acknowledgement of a quotation's source does not, though, absolve you of the infringement of copyright.

In the U.S., copyright in work created since 1978 remains in force until 50 years after the author's death. When written work is published in the U.S., it should bear a notice of copyright in the form © [year], [author's name]. Copyright registration is optional – but there are advantages in registering. U.K. readers anticipating publication in the U.S.A. are advised to consult the chapter on U.S. copyright law (by Gavin McFarlane) in the *Writers' & Artists' Yearbook*.

**What is plagiarism?**

It was once, flippantly, explained to me that if I only read one book before I wrote something, the result would probably constitute plagiarism. If I read two books, it was legitimate research. This is over-simplistic but contains a measure of common sense.

Plagiarism is the taking of the ideas, the work, the research of another, and *passing them off as your own.*

It has already been said that there can be no copyright in facts or ideas, only in the way in which the facts and ideas are expressed. But closely paraphrasing someone else's work, using the same facts and ideas in slightly different words would probably constitute plagiarism. Research may uncover many of the facts used by another writer – but there are almost certainly other facts that you can incorporate. And you must express the facts, the information *in your own way.*

A minor point: you cannot plagiarise your own work. Nor can you infringe your own copyright.

### Can I glean facts from other people's books and articles and use them in my own?

Yes, of course you can. This is research. We all do it. And you do not have to acknowledge your sources. No one expects you to re-invent the wheel or necessarily extend the bounds of human knowledge. To repeat the above comments on copyright: there is no copyright in fact.

The prudent writer does, though, check the facts gleaned from other people's publications: there is always a risk of repeating an incorrect 'fact'. For a major non-fiction book, it is worth going back to a primary source if at all possible; for general-interest magazine articles or works of fiction it may suffice to check other secondary sources.

### Can I copyright the title of my new book?

No – see above.

### I have sold an illustrated article to a magazine. Can the magazine re-use the article and the illustrations – or the illustrations alone – without my knowledge and without further payment?

Both the article and the accompanying illustrations are covered by copyright. Whether the magazine can re-use them depends on the rights that the magazine bought from you. (*See* below.) You will probably have sold the usual First British Serial Rights in the text and a single reproduction right in the illustrations. If so, the magazine cannot re-use either words or pictures without your permission – for which you should be paid.

It is quite possible that, in a busy editorial office, the re-use was done without thought and the magazine will gladly pay you for the second use. Before you take the matter up with the editor though, check the rights that the magazine acquired. If they told you that they were taking, e.g., 'All rights in both text and pictures,' and you didn't object, they are probably within their rights.

**If I submit an article to a magazine *on spec,* what is to stop the editor rejecting it, but taking the idea and noting the facts … and getting a friend or a staff writer to rewrite it?**

In theory, nothing. To repeat, there is no copyright in facts or in ideas. In practice though, despite the fears of most beginners, it seldom happens.

If you provide an editor with an interesting and well-written article, of the required length, on just the right subject at just the right time you will (usually, and with luck) get an acceptance. Editorial offices are busy places and life is too short to bother with commissioning a rewrite of someone else's otherwise acceptable article.

The belief that it happens is fostered by beginners (and others) seeing an article along the same lines as their own rejected submission, appearing in a subsequent issue of the magazine. But ideas are sparked off by many things: news items, the unusual weather, a topic of conversation, etc., and more than one freelance writer can seize on the same idea floating past in the air. And, of course, plenty of freelance writers keep tags on important upcoming dates, anniversaries, etc. An editor may have an article on the same subject as yours already in stock: the one already accepted will take precedence over yours. Freelance writers must not only be good – they also have to get lucky.

When it comes to the crunch though, confronted by two comparable articles on similar subjects, many editors will favour the tried-and-tested writer over the beginner. The answer is to make your submission better than the other's. Good luck.

# SAFEGUARDING RIGHTS – AND ADDING PICTURES

## What are Rights?

We have already explained *copyright*. The copyright in a writer's work is a potentially valuable commodity: in exchange for payment, a writer can grant *licences* to magazine and/or book publishers, to use his/her work. These licences are permission to exploit one or more *rights* – parts of the copyright.

Usually, a writer will be able to sell magazine rights, book rights or broadcasting rights. These do not overlap – i.e., the sale of broadcasting rights in a piece of work still leaves the writer the ability to sell magazine or book rights. And there are other rights – e.g., increasingly important, electronic rights. Rights can also be for specific geographical areas – British, U.S., or World.

## What is FBSR?

FBSR is a commonly used abbreviation of First British Serial Rights – one of the above-mentioned *rights* that a writer can offer. The expression means:

**First** - the magazine is being offered the right to publish the work *for the first time* in any other (local, *see* British) magazine. Note that there is no mention of 'for payment' – even if the piece is published in a small-circulation, non-paying publication, the *First* right has been used up.

**British** - the right is applicable to a magazine published in Britain. The fact that the magazine may thereafter be on sale in another country does not affect the right to publish in the second country. For example, a British magazine is on sale in Australia. A writer could still offer First Australian Serial Rights in his/her work contained in that magazine.

**Serial** - the work is offered for use in a 'serial publication', i.e., a magazine or newspaper which is on sale at regular intervals

**Rights** - a licence to publish once. The piece of work may not, without specific permission, be re-published by the magazine, in any form.

Once FBSR has been sold, a writer could offer a magazine Second British Serial Rights: this is occasionally feasible for short stories but seldom possible for articles. Along the same lines, after FBSR, First Ruritanian Serial Rights could be offered to a Ruritanian magazine. Similarly: First North American Serial Rights. If First *World* Serial Rights were sold – as some American magazines require, often for a specified period of time, to ensure their exclusivity – then the article or story cannot be re-sold other than, later, as Second Rights.

The sale of FBSR in no way precludes the subsequent sale of Book Rights – or any other non-Serial right – or vice versa. 'All Rights' however, means just what it says: ALL RIGHTS – worldwide, serial, book, broadcasting, etc. So be careful.

Among other things, I write scripts for comic-book picture-stories. The publisher of these requires 'ALL THE COPYRIGHT FOR ALL PURPOSES'. This is unusually all-embracing, but I know of no market for Second Rights in such scripts, which are very much 'written to specification', so I see no harm in relinquishing all rights. And as there is no copyright in plots, I could still re-use the plot – if I could see a use for it. Otherwise, what would I do with any retained rights?

**I have seen small magazines saying that, because they can only offer very small payments for submitted work, they 'will only take Second Rights', leaving First Rights still for sale. Is this correct?**

Absolutely not. First Rights are precisely what they say: the right to publication before anyone else in the specified geographical area.

The whole question of First and/or Second Rights is of more significance to a short story writer than to an article-writer. Second Rights in short stories are occasionally a marketable proposition; very few magazines will be interested in Second Rights in an article. But, to repeat yet again, there is no copyright in ideas or facts, so an article can always be rewritten, whereas a short story cannot. And because the individual requirements of magazines almost always differ from those of their competitors, an article usually has to be rewritten anyway, to the new magazine's style, length, etc. – creating new First Rights. I have always been prepared to relinquish virtually whatever Rights to an article are required by a magazine; and I often rewrite material.

## Should I sell World Rights?

This is for you to decide. And it will probably depend on the amount that the magazine will pay for World Rights. Some American magazines require First World Serial Rights – but as they often pay more than for example, British magazines, it is probably worth agreeing to their request. And depending on the magazines involved, and their geographical area of circulation, you might possibly be able to sell the piece again, to a British magazine – as long as you explain that First World Serial Rights have already been sold, and specify the magazine to which they were sold.

## I have sold a story with FBSR – but its use has been long delayed. Can I offer Second British Serial Rights before the first magazine actually publishes the story?

Put yourself in the position of Editor #1. How would you like it if a story you had bought for first publication, appeared first in another magazine? You'd be spitting mad.

The answer to the question is that you must await first publication before offering second. You have to recognise that some magazines have long lead times – and they also buy for stock. If the delay since your story was accepted is really long – years rather than months – you might write politely to the first editor, jogging his memory by enquiring as to when publication was likely. Whatever the response, you must wait. The story won't go out of date nor become unsaleable for quite a while. Be patient.

## Do I have to provide photographic illustrations to accompany my articles?

This varies from magazine to magazine. Some – fewer and fewer – magazines do not include illustrations at all: clearly they don't want them. Some editors require very high quality (almost always colour) illustrations and prefer to commission or seek these out themselves. Many magazines welcome 'packages' of words and pictures – both of high professional quality – but will not reject a good article for the lack of illustrations. You have to know your market.

Editorial preferences and requirements can often be determined by studying the magazine: if most of the illustrations have a separate by-line and this differs from that of the article-writer, you probably don't need to offer illustrations. Some magazines make a point of mentioning 'Illustrations by the writer' where this is the case. More and more magazines are providing 'Contributors' guidelines' – these will say whether or not illustrations are required (and in what form).

Put yourself in the position of the editor though. Two more-or-less equally-good, equally-acceptable articles come in, unsolicited. One submission is accompanied by good-quality illustrations, the other is not – the editor will have to ferret around and obtain some. Which article would you prefer – the complete, ready-to-go package or the one that you will have to work on? An editor will always prefer the package deal.

**I have no camera. Is there any way I can get photographs to illustrate my work?**

There is almost certainly a camera club somewhere near you. Approach them and see if any of the members would be interested in working with you. You would, of course, need to explain that, at least initially, you would not be *commissioning* photographs, that the photographs would be submitted *on spec* but that you would ask for a separate byline for the photographs and would arrange for payment to be appropriately apportioned. Some magazines pay for a package, others differentiate between payment for words and payment for pictures.

You might also need to make it clear that illustrations for magazine use are not the same as photographs to be submitted to a club competition. Competition photographs may well be 'artistic': for magazine use it is more important that the subject is clear, big and sharp.

Another way of obtaining photographic illustrations to accompany your articles is to seek the help of relevant commercial firms or trade organisations.

Write to the Public Relations Officer or the Press Officer at the firm or organisation's head office; state that you are writing an article about something relevant to their product/interest for speculative (or, even better, commissioned) submission to a named magazine; and if possible, ask for pictures of something very specific. You will often be lucky.

Some while ago, I wrote an article on the history of lawn-mowers, but had no suitable illustrations. Having seen an ideal photograph in another publication, credited to a lawn-mower manufacturer, I wrote to them, asking for pictures of early machines. Within a few days I received a batch of highly suitable photographs including reproductions of early advertisements and cartoons.

I submitted my article, accompanied by several of the manufacturer's illustrations – making the source clear to the editor and asking that the manufacturer be credited for them. The 'package' was accepted; the manufacturer got a 'credit' line; I got paid for the words alone. Everyone was happy. I have successfully followed the same practice with other organisations, other magazines.

You will sometimes find an ideal illustration in a museum or stately home visitors shop – a postcard perhaps. You can buy the postcard, of course. You may NOT submit this postcard with one of your articles (or as part of a non-fiction book) as a possible illustration. What you can do though, is include the postcard with your submission – making it very clear that it is not for use – with a suggestion that the editor might wish to obtain a reproduction right from the museum. The fee for this permission would be significantly more than the cost of the postcard. Do not pay the reproduction fee yourself, in advance, for a speculative submission.

If you identify a suitable illustration in an old book you *may* be able to use this as an illustration to an article or in a new book of your own. First, though, you must check that the source book and the illustration are out of copyright. And remember, the copyright period is now 70 years after the creator's death. With a really old book, you might be able to assume that – unless there is any possibility that someone else has obtained the rights to it. Be careful.

But all of the above suggestions are less than adequate alternatives. Cameras are no longer difficult to understand or use: you need do little more than 'point and click'. Nor are they particularly expensive. You should really investigate the possibility of taking your own photographs. A 35 mm 'compact' camera, maybe with a zoom lens, will be all that you need.

## Should I take colour, or black-and-white photographs to illustrate my articles?

Once again, this depends on the requirements of the individual magazines. Some magazines – notably, but not exclusively, the lower-paying ones – still use a lot of black-and-white illustrations. The trend however is inexorably towards more and more colour. You must study your markets – perhaps the most important ongoing task of any magazine-writer – and decide for yourself whether your target magazines want colour or black-and-white.

Determining that – colour or black-and-white – is relatively easy. The next option is between colour transparencies and colour prints. A lot of magazines will accept colour prints – and reproduce them in either colour or black-and-white, whichever suits their editorial requirements. With more and more magazines requiring a pre-submission article outline/query (*see* Chapter 8, page 103) it is often worth enquiring, in that, what type of colour illustrations are required.

As a rule of thumb, the more up-market, glossy magazines tend to prefer transparencies to prints. Most will accept 35 mm slides; one or two insist on a larger format.

You may be surprised at the cost of producing black-and-white photographs. The mass market is now for colour prints for which the prices have fallen sharply under competitive pressure. Black-and-white photography is now a minority, specialist, activity – and costs significantly more than holiday 'happy snapping'. (One major specialist photographic dealer was charging £7.49 in 2000, for developing and printing a black-and-white film.)

## What size do black-and-white prints need to be? What sort of (black-and-white) film should I use?

Professionals would submit 10" x 8" black-and-white prints – which look really impressive. But, unless you are going to do all your own film processing – and remember, you are primarily a writer, not a snapper – prints this size are expensive. So long as the subject of your photograph is large within the print, I would be inclined to settle for 7" x 5" black-and-white prints, unless an editor specified a larger size. You might be able to obtain these as relatively inexpensive *enprints*.

(I've even got away with submitting postcard-sized prints, but wouldn't recommend it.)

It is possible to have black-and-white prints made from colour print film. But black-and-white prints will be of better quality from black-and-white film. Unless you need to photograph a black cat in a coal cellar – for which you'd have to use the fastest film available – I recommend using a 100 ISO black-and-white film.

## What about colour film?

If you are going to submit colour prints then most of the colour print films will produce acceptable prints. I would standardise on a 200 ISO film.

If you have to produce 35 mm transparencies, I would opt for 100 ISO Fujichrome film; failing the availability of that, Kodachrome 64.

## Can I sell my photographs more than once?

Unless you come to some different arrangement – for significantly enhanced payment – it is standard practice for a magazine to buy a *single reproduction right* in a black-and-white or colour photograph. There is no question of *first* or *second* rights as would apply to your words, just one-use rights. I have sold several of my black-and-white photographs again and again.

Generally speaking, magazines are very good about returning prints and transparencies after they have used them; it is, of course, up to you to provide adequately sized and protected return envelopes – the conventional s.a.e.

## What about a camera – what sort of camera should I buy?

As mentioned above, if you have in the past been put off by the idea of coping with a camera and the confusing world of exposures, shutter speeds, apertures, etc., you can get a simple-to-use, 'point-and-click' 35 mm compact camera that will do everything for you. A compact with a zoom lens and built-in flash will do even more.

If you want to be a little bit more adventurous, a modern 35 mm single-lens reflex* (SLR) camera with zoom* lens will not cost much more – and can open up a whole new world of photography for you. The modern SLR camera – like the even simpler compact – will have automatic focusing and exposure control, automatic film loading and rewinding, yet allow you to take control as and when you wish. Many also have a built-in flash.

> * A single-lens reflex camera allows the photographer to see, via the lens, a system of reflecting surfaces [a movable mirror and a five-sided glass prism] and a ground-glass screen, exactly what the picture will include. A zoom lens allows the photographer to zoom in and out, changing the camera's view from wide angle to long-distance.

Unless you really get into the photographic side – remember, you're a writer, – I would not indulge in any more photographic equipment. Photography can be a very 'extra-gadget' oriented pastime: resist that temptation.

Equally, at least for the time being, I would recommend that you do not go for a digital camera. Certainly, there is much to be said in their favour: instant review of the picture, no film, home 'processing' (on your desktop computer and printer which, being a writer, you almost certainly already have) and picture-enhancement capability, and the facility to transmit your photographs by e-mail. But, as yet, the resolution – roughly, the size and closeness of the dots that make up the picture – of low- and medium-priced digital cameras is not good enough for magazine reproduction. Suitable high-resolution, digital cameras are mega-expensive. For now, stick to old-fashioned film cameras.

### How do I go about taking saleable photographs?

Perhaps the most important advice is to remember that, having bought a camera, you must USE it. Relatively speaking, film is cheap. Take a lot of pictures and discard many (80 per cent?). Just use the good ones.

That apart, a few 'ground rule' suggestions:

- Decide on the subject – and although that sounds obvious, it is too often overlooked by beginners – and then fill the picture *in the viewfinder* with that, and that alone. If you do not compose your picture in the viewfinder you will have to resort to selective enlarging of the real content of your picture.
- Get in close – which is, of course, the same important advice expressed differently.
- Watch the background – everyone knows about, and avoids, the tree growing out of the subject's head, but any 'fussy' background can spoil a picture, particularly a colour one. Aim for a contrasting background against which the subject stands out – dark subject against light background or vice versa. Remember that you can squat down, setting a subject against a background of sky, or stand on something and have a background of grass. And, to be a tad technical, a wide-aperture long-focus lens focused on a close-up subject can throw the background nicely out of focus.
- Emphasise the diagonal as a composition aid – and recognise that the four one-third points (i.e., one third of the frame up or down and one-third in from either side) attract attention – position important parts of a subject at these points. Avoid positioning any subject dead-centre.
- Whenever possible, include people in your pictures. Ideally, have them doing something – and concentrating on what they are doing, not staring at the camera. The three-quarter side view of someone's head and shoulders, dominating the foreground, looking *into* the picture will also often improve, and give *scale* to, an otherwise unimpressive landscape.
- Be sure it's SHARP.
- Take upright pictures upright and landscape pictures landscape. The camera can be turned around. Too many beginners take all their pictures horizontally.

**What about captions for my pictures?**

It's up to you to provide them. Remember the advice to fledgling journalists: you need, as appropriate, the answers to the six basic questions. Who? What? Why?

Where? When? and How? An editor can always cut a caption down but can't always fill out an incomplete one. Some people will *only* look at the pictures and read the captions. You've got to accommodate their needs too.

Some editors, and some writers, prefer to stick (typed, of course) captions to the back of their photographic prints. If you go down this road, the caption should also include a key-word from the associated article title and, of course, the writer's name and address. Even if a colleague provides the photographs, it is probably most convenient if all editorial contact is with the writer. But you might consider adding a sticker with the photographer's name and address, just in case.

Unless an editor specifies differently, I prefer to mark the back of a print with a key-word (as before) and an identification number for the picture (and, of course, my name and address on a sticky label) and provide a list of captions on a separate sheet. This separate sheet approach is the only sensible method for captioning colour transparencies. I use the film processor's numbers on the slide mounts as identification numbers, if necessary also giving the date – which is also on the mount.


**I have written a book for children. Do I have to provide the illustrations for it? (I have a friend who can draw beautiful pictures.)**

Unless you are, or your friend is, an artist of professional ability and thoroughly *au fait* with commercial artwork and printing techniques, don't even attempt to illustrate your book. Apart from the fact that much non-professional artwork *looks* amateurish, and could even damn the accompanying manuscript unseen, most publishers have their own 'stable' of freelance artists who they prefer to illustrate their books.

With a story book, the publisher has first to decide how many illustrations he can afford; the second decision – an editorial one – is to determine which scenes are to be depicted. The writer will not necessarily be involved in either decision.

There are some cases – e.g., children's picture-books – where the 'content' of each illustration is important to the story. A brief description of the required picture is then appropriate and maybe even a very rough sketch – for clarification purposes only. It is important not to give *too much*, too detailed, instruction to the artist: artists (and publishers' editors) like to exercise their own creativity without undue restrictions.

If you write picture-stories for children's comics (or the longer graphic novels) the same advice applies. The writer provides the dialogue, thoughts, and captions which are incorporated within the individual frames or panels – and a description of what the picture is to show. The editor 'adjusts' the text and artist's briefing; the artist draws the pictures.

**I am writing a non-fiction book. I want this to include a number of diagrams, flow-charts and maps. Do I have to produce these – if so, how, in what form?**

First, because it is always highly desirable that a non-fiction book author sells his/her book before it is written – i.e., on the basis of an agreed synopsis plus sample chapters – this question is one you should take up with the publisher.

If you write a complete non-fiction book without a publisher's prior commitment, you run the considerable risk that *the ideal* publisher may like the book a lot, but not the way you've written it. Rewriting is a pain. It's better to sort it out first. For further advice on the initiating of a non-fiction book, consult my *How To Write Non-Fiction Books – see* Chapter 2.

It is likely that your publisher will be happy with either finished, but un-lettered, line drawings, or 'roughs' – rough sketches.

Few authors will be capable of producing finished 'book quality' drawings. Line drawings – particularly maps – produced for other purposes will very seldom be right for reproduction in a book: the thickness of the lines, the amount of detail and the lettering will all be wrong. Even if you are a competent draughtsman and have re-drawn your illustrations, your lettering will seldom be just what the publisher requires.

So, if you are a draughtsman, agree with the publisher on the size to make the line-drawings (this may be 50 or 100 per cent larger than the eventual reproduced size) and on the minimum line-thickness, bearing in mind that these too will be reduced. Then draw them.

When I have produced line drawings for my technical books, I have been able to fit these onto standard A4 sheets – and I have often used an ordinary *brand-new* fibre-tip pen to draw them. (A Rotring, or similar draughtsman's pen is better.) I do not do the lettering. I photocopy the finished line drawing and mark all the required lettering, in colour, on the photocopy – as a guide to the artist.

If you don't feel up to that amount of artistry, go for producing 'roughs'. These can be simple pencil drawings – but don't make them *too* rough. Ideally, draw them accurately to line and scale, and 50 or 100 per cent larger, so that the artist can trace them, in ink.

# 6

# EXERCISING YOUR IMAGINATION

**Most published short stories seem to be in women's magazines, and are usually romance-oriented. Is there any market for more traditional, 'mainstream' short stories?**

Without doubt, most short stories appear in women's magazines – but they are not all *merely* romance-oriented. The use of the word *merely* is not in any way to put down romantic short stories – after all, they say that love makes the world go round, don't they? – but to emphasise that in many stories, the romance is only an element in the story. Also women's magazines often use ghost stories, 'soft' crime stories and twist-in-the-tail stories – often with no love interest at all.

If you want to make money from your short story writing, there are, apart from the women's magazines, only a few markets. The most important – i.e., the one probably paying the highest – 'other' market in the UK, is currently the bi-monthly *World Wide Writers*. This chunky paperback sized magazine operates on a competitive basis: writers submit their 2,500–5,000-word stories together with an entry form (from the magazine) and a reading fee of £6 (or US$10); all stories submitted during each 2-monthly competition period are read and judged; around a dozen of the submitted stories are used in each issue, with prizes ranging from a minimum of £125 ($200) to £625 ($1,000). And there is an additional £3,000 ($5,000) prize for the year's best story. Every rejected story receives a nine-point *critique*.

OK, so it's a competition-based market rather than a conventional magazine – and there can be only one big winner. But isn't every story submitted to any magazine *in competition* – with every other story submitted to that magazine? If your story gets accepted, you've won the prize (of paid publication). The only real difference is that *World Wide Writers* charge a reading fee – for which you get a *critique* which you certainly wouldn't get from a mainstream magazine editor.

If you don't want to write for the women's magazines, *World Wide Writers* is worth investigating. They will send you a free sample copy if you write to them, at PO Box 3229, Bournemouth BH1 1ZS. Website: www.users.globalnet.co.uk/~writ-intl (In America, contact World Writers USA, PO Box 267, Edgewater, MD 21037-0267. Website: www.worldwriters.net)

But there are also a few conventional mainstream other-than-women's magazines which use short stories. Investigate the magazines aimed at more mature readers – e.g., *Active Life*, *Choice* and *Yours*. Investigate the *genre* magazines – e.g., *Crimewave* and *Interzone*. They pay less than the women's magazines but at least they pay.

Then, if publication is of greater importance to you than payment, investigate the wide range of small press ('independent') magazines around. They come and go and seldom pay, other than with a few free copies, but their standards are, on the whole, very high. The best guide to the world's independent magazine field is itself an independent small press bi-monthly magazine – *Zene*. Subscribe to it for £12 (US$24) per year. Write to TTA Press, 5 Martins Lane, Witcham, Ely, Cambs CB6 2LB. Website: www.tta-press.freewire.co.uk

No beginning writer of fiction should overlook short story competitions. Most of the writing magazines run them from time to time – and the set story subjects are usually other than romance.

Remember though, there is no reason why men shouldn't write short stories for the women's magazines. They can use a pen-name if preferred. Not all the stories are romantic … and the pay is definitely better. It IS the biggest market.


**My short stories tend to be rather long – some as much as 10,000 words – while published stories seem to be getting shorter. What can I do?**


You are quite right in your observation of the current trends. Stories are certainly getting shorter. People have less time to sit and read. There are too many competing attractions.

The most practical advice I can offer you is: learn to write shorter.

There is virtually no market at all for 10,000 word stories: 4–5,000 is about the most that is acceptable anywhere today – and 2,500 is the most popular length for the longer story. You will find that the payment per word is usually far higher for a

1,000-word 'short-short' than it is for a longer one – they're harder to write. Remember the witty wisdom of George Bernard Shaw who, apologising for the length of a letter, explained that he had not had the time to write a shorter one.

Study the market. Study the stories that are being published today. Notice how they omit much descriptive material and cut to the basic story; notice how quickly they get into the action. Many (unpublished) short stories would benefit from cutting out the first several paragraphs, sometimes even the first several pages.

One final comment on the subject of extra-long 'short' stories. Some years ago, my favourite science fiction writer, Anne McCaffrey wrote and published several quite long short stories in what were then classed as 'pulp' magazines. I notice that in recent years she has incorporated and extended some of these into full-length SF novels. Maybe you can do something similar. (Her 8,000-word story, *Lady in the Tower*, first appeared in the *Magazine of Fantasy and Science Fiction* in April 1959. It is now a major element within *The Rowan* published in Great Britain in 1990.)

**I have had several short stories published. I would now like to make them into a book. Will a publisher be interested, or should I self-publish?**

First, congratulations on your successes. I'm afraid, though, that I can't be very encouraging about your wish to make the stories into a book. Unless you are already a really big 'name' – and that for novels, rather than for short stories – it will be extremely difficult to find a publisher willing to take an anthology of your stories. I don't think publishers actually like taking books of short stories, even from their own 'names', but they probably feel that they have to, from them. The accepted publishing *wisdom* is that books of short stories don't sell.

The same message would – certainly should – apply equally to self-publishing which also involves all the other problems of self-publishing (*see* Chapter 10). I should give up the idea.

**I make up a story every night for my grandchildren. They think the stories are great – and their parents say that I should get them published. How can I do this?**

Story-telling is a great gift. Cherish it. And keep up the good work.

Publication? Maybe. I suggest that you start by writing short stories for children and offering them to grown-up magazines that feature a children's short-short story spot. *People's Friend* springs immediately to mind. The magazine is targeted at people of mature years, and the stories – which are only 5–600 words each – are therefore probably meant for grandchildren. Investigate too the several children's magazines: most of these include a short story.

But there are differences between stories for telling and stories for reading: you may need to polish up your story-*writing* skills.

I have to add a word of warning though. Young children enjoy 'prime time' attention from parents and grandparents: because you are telling a story just for them, they will enjoy it even more. They are going to be far less critical than … for example, the editor of a weekly magazine. But if you will **WORK** at your children's stories, you could get them published.

**I have heard it said that romance novels are written to 'a formula'. What is the formula?**

There is no formula.

Inevitably though, there is a degree of predictability about a romance. By its very nature, a romance novel is about the gradual blossoming of a relationship between a woman and a man – from first meeting, through development, to eventual happy ending. And, as everyone knows, the path of true love never did run smooth – so there will be ups and downs in the relationship. Other characters will make their entrances and their exits with varying influence on the two main protagonists. But every reader knows that, in the end, all will work out satisfactorily: these are present-day fairy stories. If that is a formula, you have it.

More important than any so-called formula though, is the need for the characters to come alive and for the action to be realistic and believable. Publishers will be looking for a fresh and original approach within their guidelines – and for high-quality storytelling.

The setting of a romance novel is also important. If much of the story takes place in an exotic tropical country this will seem more exciting, to a Briton or an

American, than a story set in the back streets of Brighton or Boston. But romance novels sell in a global marketplace: to a Filipino reader, Brighton may seem strange and fascinating; to a reader in Japan, a Welsh mountain setting might be far more exotic than a beach in Hawaii.

Whatever the setting though, it is essential that everything you write about it is accurate. Even the most exotic setting is someone's backyard – and they'll surely let you know if you get it wrong.

Because most readers of romance novels are women, and because most readers want to identify with the heroine, the stories are usually told throughout in the third person, from the heroine's viewpoint. The viewpoint will often be specified by the publisher. But these are guidelines and constraints rather than a formula.

All of that said, there are often a few more constraints and requirements. Some publishers – mainly the American ones – issue guidelines or 'tipsheets' for their authors.

These guidelines may specify the age of the heroine and the slightly older hero, and the degree of sexual explicitness. Most too, will specify the overall length that the book should be. This is because many romance imprints are geared to a fixed, low, retail price, to achieve which the books are produced in a standard format. Harlequin Mills & Boon, the major British romance publisher – who do provide authors' guidelines – specifies a book length of 50-55,000 words for some of its several series, 70,000 for others.

## What exactly is a plot – do I need to have one?

A plot is the storyline of a novel; it is the author's pre-prepared plan of how the story will develop, from opening scene to final solution – the pre-construction blueprint. It is in the plot that the author dreams up and sets down all the conflicts and problems that the characters are going to have to overcome on their way to THE END.

Some authors suggest that they do not plot their novels in advance. They begin with an intriguing scene or some startling dialogue, and then travel hopefully therefrom. (In my experience, most such 'hopeful travellers' seem to be those who write the more 'literary' or 'straight' novels, rather than the better-selling genre novels. Which may explain the sales figures.) They say that they already know their characters well and that they let them develop their own story. When quizzed on this approach to storytelling some admit that although they don't have a fully-fledged plot written down, they do have a good idea, at the back of their minds, of where the story will be going, and roughly how it's going to get there.

One can only admire those authors who will start on their 100,000-word journey without a 'route map' – and undoubtedly some very successful authors do work in this way. For most of us though, it is useful to know where we are going and what the peaks and troughs are, along the way.

Certainly, for a first novel, it would be prudent to develop your storyline before starting to write the *book proper*. In any case, the plot is not written on tablets of stone; if you want to change the storyline as the writing progresses, there is nothing to prevent you giving yourself permission. But having the plot to start from will enable you to appreciate the consequences of such changes.

### How do I develop/prepare a plot for my novel?

Every author has his/her own method of developing a plot – but there is a certain consistency at the core of most methods.

First, think about the **theme** of your novel. The theme is one of those hard-to-define concepts but basically it's what the book is about. It might be just a word or two, like 'child abuse', or a clichéd phrase like 'money is at the root of all evil'. Once you have established your theme, you will be better able to plot your novel to illustrate it.

Because your novel will be all about people (unless it's a new *Watership Down*, but the same principles will apply anyway) you need to establish at least your main characters before you start. And you need to really *know* those characters – much of the plot will depend on how they will react to the circumstances that confront them.

Preparing a brief but detailed biography of each of the main characters is a useful way of getting to know them. Think about – and record – their age (with birthdate and star sign, perhaps) and appearance, where they live, their family and educational background, their likes and dislikes in food, drink, clothes, music and people, and, generally what makes them tick. (*See* also Chapter 3, page 33.)

So you know what your novel is about and who the main protagonists are to be. And you've got a vague idea of the story you are going to tell. Now you can think about the plot. Several authors have separately suggested this approach. It worked for them, it can work for you.

Take a sheet of paper and down the left-hand side, number the lines from 1 to 20. Each numbered line will represent one of the chapters in your novel. There is nothing sacrosanct about that 20, it merely represents the average number of chapters in an average-length novel. If you want to make it 15 or 25, feel free – it's your novel you're planning.

On line 1, bearing in mind the need to introduce the leading characters early on and, indeed, to establish what type of story your novel is to be, make a brief note of the scene. Now go to line 20 and make a note of how the book will end. I really like Dick Winfield's comment in his *One Way To Write Your Novel* that if, before you start, you don't know what the end will be, 'You'll not be writing a novel. You'll only be improving your typing speed.'

With lines 1 and 20 duly annotated, it is time to exercise your imagination. On each line, make a note of what will happen in that chapter. Plan the 'ups and downs', identify where a new character is to be introduced – make sure that something significant is happening in each chapter. If nothing much happens – you don't need that chapter. Each chapter must move the story along.

You don't have to complete all the chapter-line notes in one go; fill some of them in and then go off for a think. And/or a drink. Plot at your own pace. No one's chasing you for a result.

Remember that unless there is conflict – between one character and another, between a character and his/her own conscience, between a character and the environment, etc. – there is no story. If everything goes smoothly, that's boring. Keep putting difficulties in the way of the protagonists. A famous crime writer once remarked that when he couldn't think what to do next in his plot, he had a door open and a man appear, firing a gun. That's the right attitude. Fiction has to be more exciting than real life.

Once the 20 chapter-lines are complete – and you are reasonably happy with what they show – expand on your notes, chapter by chapter. Develop the conflicts and their resolutions – are the resolutions realistic and believable? Have the protagonists behaved *in character*? Are the times, dates, seasons and settings *consistent*?

**What is a synopsis? Why do publishers so often ask for one? Having given a publisher a synopsis, can I depart from it in the eventual novel?**

A synopsis is just what the dictionary says it is: a summary. It needs to outline, to the prospective publisher, the storyline of the novel you are offering.

But that sounds very much like the same description as you gave for the plot? True. They both outline the way your story is going/to go. It's helpful to think of the plot as your working plan and of the synopsis as the summary that sells the storyline to the publisher. More specifically, the synopsis is your sales pitch.

The synopsis needs to outline the complete story but in a way that attracts the publisher. And it's really important that the synopsis outlines the COMPLETE story: to omit the final twist or denouement defeats the whole object of it. The publisher has to know that the story will work: without the concluding climax it won't. The synopsis needs to be logical and complete – understandable to someone else. The plot need only be understandable by you.

The synopsis should introduce the main characters and settings, and include brief details of the major scenes that make up the story. It should detail the basic, overall conflict, the back-story disclosure, the secondary conflicts and their resolutions; and most important of all, the scene that *determines* the final climax as well as the climactic one itself.

Some authors include brief samples of the main characters' dialogue within the synopsis – no more than the odd sentence – but because the synopsis is almost invariably accompanied by about three sample chapters, the need for this is questionable.

The synopsis has to demonstrate to the publisher that your novel will have sufficient *content* and *texture*. The synopsis has to demonstrate the *shape* of your novel: show that it will have a gripping beginning, that it will retain a reader's attention in the middle – and will have a satisfactory and believable end.

It has to do all of the above in a concise document. Some authors suggest that the synopsis should be about 2 per cent of the length of the eventual novel. A planned 100,000-word novel would therefore have a synopsis of about 2,000 words long – four or five pages of single-spaced typescript. Shorter is usually better than longer – just as long as it serves its purpose well.

Because the synopsis – and certainly the plot – is (usually) written before the novel itself there is always the possibility that you will wish/need to diverge from it when actually writing. You may discover that some of the details don't *quite* work out right, or maybe you decide that one of the lesser characters should take on a more important role. No publisher will object to such changes. It's your novel. Just as long as the storyline still works and is not **too** different from the synopsis.

### What is 'writer's block' – and what is the cure for it?

Writer's block is that awful state when you sit looking at a blank computer screen or blank sheet of paper … and can't think what to write next. It can be when you are thinking about starting your next piece of work. There are a number of suggested remedies for the absence of basic ideas (*see* Chapter 2). Equally, it can be when you are mid-novel and can't think how to extricate your hero from the perilous situation you have got him into. Or how to get him into it in the first place. Basically, you're stuck.

Notice that I said 'mid-novel'. As a non-fiction author, I believe that writer's block is very largely a problem faced by novelists. Writing a non-fiction book, I always work to a detailed synopsis which has been pre-agreed by the publisher who has commissioned the book on that basis. I always know what I am next going to write about – it's all down there in the synopsis. (And if I don't feel particularly enthusiastic about 'the next' topic in my non-fiction synopsis, there's nothing to stop me from writing about some other, more 'attractive', synopsis topic today, and coming back to the omitted topic later.)

Novelists – largely those writing *genre* novels – who have had to produce detailed synopses seem to have less trouble with writer's block. They have a storyline – a plot – to which they are working. Like the non-fiction author, they always know where they are heading … and usually, how they are going to get there.

So-o-o, the cure for writer's block. First and foremost, I believe the carefully worked out storyline/plot/synopsis is the best preventative. But that advice is no help if you're well into an un-planned novel … and blocked. For that situation, some suggestions:

- When you stop working each day, stop in mid-scene and mid-sentence.
- Instead of merely re-reading the last page that you wrote – as is basic common sense for any writer, – actually type out again the last page. This will often get you going again.
- If really stuck whilst more or less in mid-flow, try writing anything – any old non-productive rubbish. Something to get the juices flowing again. Describe the spots on the study carpet or the weather outside. Or even just type out your name and address repeatedly. With luck you'll quickly get fed up with the sight of it and move on. Maybe write a dialogue between your two main characters describing the blocked situation you've got them into: have them discuss various solutions, no matter how way out.
- Have a cup of coffee, or tea – or one or more large, strong whiskies. The alcoholic solution will at least make you feel better, temporarily. Or phone a friend and explain your problem. Talking or writing about your problem often suggests a solution.
- Give up and go for a walk – it'll all look different/better tomorrow.

**Is it all right to write my suspense novel in the first person? I have been told that writing from a third person's viewpoint is more 'suitable'.**

It's your novel – write it from whichever viewpoint you like, as long as it 'works'. That said, apart from a deep-seated personal belief that writing in the third person is easier than writing in the first person, the third person viewpoint is more usual for any *genre* novel. Against that, of course, maybe the suspense will feel more real when described in the first person.

It is ALWAYS best to 'show, rather than tell'. That is, have your characters act out a scene themselves rather than having another describe what occurred.

A big problem/disadvantage of writing in the first person is you can only write descriptively about the things seen or done by that person. Anything else becomes mere hearsay. In a full-length novel it is quite usual to write from more than one person's viewpoint, opening the story up to a greater wealth of knowledge and experience. There's no reason why there shouldn't be several first or several third person's viewpoints, although a mix of first and third person's viewpoints would be unusual. Beware too many different viewpoints though – and do make sure it is clear whose viewpoint you are writing from, at any point in the story. Separate different viewpoints by an extra line space.

**What *sort* of novel should I write, i.e., in which *genre*?**

You should write whatever sort of novel you like.

This will probably best be within the *genre* you usually read. And in this context, specifically, I am using the word *genre* to include 'straight' or 'literary' novels as well as the various categories of 'popular' fiction: crime, thriller, science-fiction, romance, etc. Whatever your choice though, it is important that you do not attempt to force yourself into working in a *genre* with which you are uncomfortable. The writing world is full of beginners who, bewitched by the reported riches earned by, say, romance authors, attempt – and fail – to write a romance which, deep down, they feel is 'beneath them' and which they would not normally deign to read.

All of the above is common sense. You will always write better when you enjoy what you are writing.

However, reverting to the usual distinction between 'straight'/literary and *genre* fiction, the first novelist will have more chance of getting a *genre* novel accepted than a literary one. Merely by browsing around chain bookstore shelves, it is obvious that the general public buy many more *genre* novels than 'straight' novels.

Beware 'creative writing' tutors who pour scorn on *genre* writing.

**Can I write my own novel about the characters in another author's novel?**

Unless the 'original' novel is out of copyright, without express permission – NO. To do so could be classed as 'passing off' – i.e., offering something which may appear to be written by the original author, thereby unlawfully cashing in on his/her success.

Permitted exceptions:

- For the period of the copyright, a dead author's work is part of his/her estate: the executors and the publishers may authorise further books about the estate's established characters to increase the estate's earnings. E.g., several James Bond books were written after the death of his creator, Ian Fleming.
- A publisher may establish a series of books about a set of characters, the books sometimes – but not necessarily – apparently written by a single author. Such books are often written by a number of commissioned authors, specifically about the established characters. As an author new to that publisher, you could offer them – and only them – a storyline about their characters and hope for a commission – but you would be unwise to write much without the commission.
- Not novels, but comic-magazine picture-script story characters are usually 'owned' by the magazine publishers. Anyone writing for that magazine may submit scripts about those characters – but only to the owning magazine.

**Recommended further reading**

*How to Write Stories for Magazines*, Donna Baker
   (Allison & Busby, London, 1986, revised 1995.)
*The Craft of Novel-Writing*, Dianne Doubtfire
   (Allison & Busby, London, 1978, revised 1998.)
*Writing for Children*, Allan Frewin Jones and Lesley Pollinger
   (Teach Yourself Books, London, 1996.)
*How to Write for Children*, Tessa Krailing
   (Allison & Busby, London, 1988, revised 1996.)
*How to Plot Your Novel*, Jean Saunders
   (Allison & Busby, London, 1999.)
*The Craft of Writing Romance*, Jean Saunders
   (Writers' Bookshop, Peterborough, 2000.)

*How to Write Short-Short Stories*, Stella Whitelaw
    (Allison & Busby, London, 1996.)
*How to Write & Sell a Book Proposal*, Stella Whitelaw
    (Writers' Bookshop, Peterborough, 2000.)

# 7

# AGENTS, AGREEMENTS AND ADVANCES

**Do I need a literary agent?**

The answer to this depends on what you write – fiction or non-fiction, short pieces for magazines or book-length works – and to some extent, on how prolific you are.

If you write non-fiction articles for magazines you should always write for a specific target market and, increasingly, you will have sought and obtained editorial interest or a commission before you start. (*See* Chapter 8.) There is neither need nor room for an agent in this process. And if you are in the fortunate position of having editors seeking you out to write for them, on *your* subject, again, they will contact you direct without need for an agent. Furthermore, being aware of this situation, few agents would take on a feature-article writer as a client.

If you write mostly short stories, and with the objective of earning money from your writing, you will probably have to write mostly for women's magazines. The reason for the 'earning money' qualification is that there are only a few reasonable paying markets for short stories other than women's magazines. As with feature articles, the requirements of each magazine differ subtly from their competitors; increasingly the short story needs to be geared to the specific market.

Once again, there is only limited scope for a literary agent to operate usefully; other than as a favour to a treasured novelist client, most agents would hesitate long before taking on the handling of a writer's short stories.

There is currently one exception to that comment: an agency called Midland Exposure is prepared to take on short story writers and is having considerable success. For a fee, they offer their clients constructive advice which often leads to future sales. Contact them at 4 Victoria Court, Oadby, Leicester LE2 4AF – or e-mail: partners@midlandexposure.co.uk. Understandably, they take a larger percentage of their clients' earnings than do other agents who deal mainly with novels – that pay better.

If you write specialist non-fiction books – such as how-to books like this, academic texts, or books about crafts and hobbies of limited interest – you will have researched and know the few relevant likely publishers. Having approached these likely publishers with details of your proposed book, with luck and persistence, the book will have been commissioned. An agent doesn't come into this scenario and many agents would hesitate to take on projects of such narrow interest.

A general interest non-fiction book, however – such as the story of how you rowed single-handed across the Atlantic or a history of the football World Cup – would be a different matter. It is quite possible that, once the (forthcoming) availability of such a book became known, several publishers would approach the author seeking to buy the book. In such a situation – where an auction might develop and where a number of different rights (*see* Chapter 5) might be available to offer – then the services of an agent would be invaluable. Indeed, agents would probably seek out the author, offering their services.

A literary agent is also of considerable assistance and advantage to the novelist. Many publishers *say* that they will only look at new fiction submitted by reputable agents. If however, these publishers were to 'come across' a seemingly spectacular and potentially bestselling novel directly, i.e., unagented, they would be most unlikely to turn it away.

Part of the reason for publishers' preference for agented submissions is the staff cut-backs that were a feature of the latter part of the 20th Century. There is a vast amount of, usually unproductive, work in sifting through the 'slush pile' – the many unsolicited novels offered to publishers. Many publishers would think themselves lucky if they were able to accept even one per cent of the 'slush pile' submissions. By insisting on agented submissions only, the mass of unpublishable and/or incorrectly targeted material is filtered out – by the agents – before the publishers need to look at anything. Agents save publishers money.

But an agent is by no means always needed by a novelist. There are still many – often smaller – publishers who are happy to deal with authors direct. And certainly a number of successful authors who are well versed in business negotiations and who know their way around the world of publishers, choose not to be represented by agents.

Apart from a writer's need for an agent, it is also useful to be aware of the problems involved in a writer *getting* an agent.

A fledgling writer cannot just write to an agent and expect, as of right, to be taken on as a client. An agent will only accept as a client a writer in whom he/she has faith and confidence. An agent's income derives from a percentage of the writer's earnings: non-existent writing earnings mean non-existent income for the agent to compensate for the often considerable work of trying to sell the writer's work.

It can be as difficult to find an agent to take you on, as it is to find a publisher to accept your work.

## What will an agent do for me?

A good agent can be a godsend to a writer. An agent can guide a writer into more profitable writing areas; an agent can encourage a writer and help in maintaining possible flagging confidence; an agent can sometimes offer a shoulder for the writer to cry on; an agent can offer pre-submission editorial advice.

An agent knows which publisher is thinking of launching a new imprint and is looking for a particular type of novel. An agent knows of an about-to-be-launched series of non-fiction books – and of the specialisms of his/her 'stable' of clients; the agent can recommend a client-writer to the series editor. An agent gets to hear about publishers in difficulties or doing well – where to take a new book and where not to. Agents develop relationships with editors: they need each other.

But above all, an agent can remove from the writer the worries of business negotiation. An agent knows, and works to obtain, the best terms the writer-client can expect: an agent won't ask for the unattainable financial moon, but will get as far towards it as possible. An agent knows about subsidiary rights – other sales that the writer might never think of. It would be a poor agent – or one working for an unusually skilled and businesslike writer-negotiator – who couldn't increase a client's income by more than the agent's percentage.

An agent wants the very best deal he/she can get for the client: the agent gets a fixed percentage of that best deal.

## How do I get myself an agent?

As mentioned above, it is often as – or more – difficult to get an agent as it is to find a publisher.

There are three basic ways to *start* on the process of finding and getting signed up with an agent:

- You can attend a talk given by an agent – agents are frequent guest speakers at writers' conferences, etc. – find their attitude or personality compatible, and make contact with them after the talk; the agent may invite you to write in.
- You can talk to already agented writers and get a recommendation – following up on which, you have to write.
- You can read through the list of agents in one of the standard writers' handbooks, seeking an agent who *looks* appropriate to your needs – or simply close your eyes and stick a pin in the list – and write to them.

But the above methods are only the start of the process; they will barely get you to first base.

You now have to convince/persuade the agent that you are a writer with sales potential – that you are, or will develop into, a working writer. You have to *sell* yourself and your writing. You have to demonstrate enthusiasm. If you're not enthusiastic about your writing, how can you expect others to enthuse about it on your behalf?

Your letter to the selected agent should introduce you, explaining your writing experience and background and giving an indication of your future writing plans and ideas. If you have already been writing successfully for some while, it would be useful to incorporate much of this material in a separate CV. But the letter should still enthuse.

If you have already made an initial contact with the agent – the first method, above – you will know that the chosen agent probably likes to see the FIRST few chapters of your novel plus a detailed synopsis. If you are a non-fiction author, the detailed synopsis plus a statement of the book's objective and assessment of the competition should probably best be accompanied by just a couple of sample chapters, but *not* the introduction. *See* Chapter 9.

When writing 'cold' to an agent (the second and third methods above) it may initially be wisest to send no more than the introductory letter, perhaps accompanied by the synopsis – and check how prepared the agent is to read your sample chapters. Have the samples ready for immediate delivery once the agent expresses a willingness to review.

In all initial correspondence with agents, be sure to enclose an adequately sized and pre-paid stamped addressed envelope. Omission of the *s,a.e.* is likely to result in your material being ignored or even binned. And some agents may ask for a reading fee – *see* below.

## Do I have to pay an agent to read my work?

A few agents ask for a fee for the initial reading of a writer's work – this is often refunded when the writer's work is placed. Most agents' entries in the standard writers' handbooks clearly specify 'No reading fee.' Members of the Association of Authors' Agents are committed to a code of practice – and do not charge a reading fee. It is therefore not difficult to avoid the few fee-chargers.

You should not, though, expect an agent who is prepared to read your work for free, in the hope that you might become an earning client, to also give you a free criticism of your work. All that you can expect from the agent who does not take you on is, 'I'm sorry, this is not for me.'

If you wish to have your work criticised and are prepared to pay for the privilege, then there are a number of people who advertise reading and criticism services. Most of the writers' magazines carry a selection of such advertisements. Some of the people offering these services have a wealth of practical experience in the editing and publishing world and/or have been well published. Others are less experienced or just unsuccessful and have taken to criticism as an easy option.

Choose a criticism service with care. And remember that anything useful seldom comes cheap.

## How much will an agent charge me?

Agents make their living from charging their client-authors a percentage of their writing earnings. This percentage is usually in the range from 10 to 15 per cent for U.K. earnings. A larger percentage – often 20 per cent – is deducted in respect of overseas earnings. This is because a home-based agent usually has to work with an overseas agent – and they will share the higher fee.

## I have already shown my book to several publishers – who have turned it down. Need I tell an agent that, when I ask them to represent me?

Simple answer: yes. The agent would not usually wish to re-offer your work to a publisher who has already turned it down. To do so accidentally could easily damage the agent's reputation and you would be most unpopular. Just occasionally though, the agent might wish to re-offer the work to one of the original publishers who rejected it – but must be aware of the earlier offer.

## What is an Agreement?

An Agreement is the contract made between the publisher and the author of a book. In it, the publisher agrees to publish the author's book and the author agrees to grant the publisher a licence to 'print, publish and sell' the book. The licence can be terminated if the book is not kept in print.

Of possibly greater interest to the author, the Agreement sets out the terms and conditions of the publication: the duties and responsibilities of both publisher and author, when the book will be published, what rate of royalties will be paid and when, the advance against royalties, the handling and distribution of subsidiary rights, and how any author/publisher disputes will be settled. If the book manuscript was not complete when the Agreement was signed – a normal situation with non-fiction books – the delivery date and book length will also be specified.

A publisher's Agreement is a specialised legal document; few High Street solicitors have the expertise to vet the document and are likely to worry expensively about the wrong, unimportant, details. The Society of Authors (*see* Chapter 2) will check and advise on members' Agreements – and a new author can join the Society before signing that first Agreement. It's well worth it.

**What are royalties?**

A royalty is a payment by the publisher to the author in respect of each copy of the book that is sold. Outside of the book publishing world, a royalty can be paid in respect of each performance of a work or each sale of a recording or similar. In the book world, royalties are usually a percentage of the book's price or of the publisher's receipts.

In the past, royalties were nearly always paid as a percentage of the *list price* – i.e., the price at which the book is listed, and which is usually marked on the book. With booksellers demanding seemingly ever-larger discounts – and the demise of the Net Book Agreement, which precluded selling books to the public at less than the listed price – some publishers now base the royalties on the net amount they receive from the bookseller. This receipts basis is said to facilitate the publisher's accounting procedures; it is of no disadvantage to the writer provided that the royalty rate is adjusted appropriately (*see* royalty rates, below).

The contract, or Agreement, which the publisher and the author – or the author's agent – negotiate and sign will specify the royalty terms.

**How much am I likely to be paid in royalties?**

Royalty rates are negotiable. But there are fairly common standard rates applicable across the industry. 'Ordinary' writers tend to be paid 'standard' royalty rates.

A 10 per cent royalty on the list price of a hardback book – fiction or non-fiction – is fairly standard. The usual royalty rate for *trade paperbacks* (books like this), which usually sell only a few thousand copies, is 7.5 to 8 per cent; for *mass market paperbacks*, which sell in the tens of thousands, the rate is usually around 5 per cent and sometimes quite a bit lower. These rates are all based on the book's list price.

Consider now the effect of basing the rates on publisher's receipts. The author of a hardback book listed at £10 would receive a £1 royalty based on 10 per cent of the list price. The large bookselling chains frequently demand (and get) a discount of at least 50 per cent on the books they buy. That is, they would pay the publisher £5 for the aforementioned £10 hardback. Were the publisher and the author to have agreed to the same 10 per cent royalty on receipts, the poor author would only receive a 50 pence royalty. Clearly, to allow for the different royalty basis, the rate should be doubled, to 20 per cent of the receipts. And the discounts demanded by supermarket chains – now also selling mass market books – can frequently exceed the 50 per cent used in the above example. The prudent author should think in terms of a doubled royalty rate if based on receipts.

If a book sells well, the publisher will recoup his fixed costs (e.g., editing, type-setting, design, etc.) and make a larger profit per book from the ensuing sales. The Agreement between author and publisher usually acknowledges this and allows for an increased rate of royalties after a specified number of sales.

Royalty jumps will vary from book to book, publisher to publisher. But they are negotiable. As a very rough indication – to get you into the right 'ball park' – the first jump might occur at 3,000 hardback sales, 10,000 trade paperback sales and 20,000 mass market paperback sales. The first jump is usually of the order of 2.5 per cent on the list price – and should therefore be about 5 per cent on receipts.

An author should not expect too much from the often attractive-looking royalty jumps though; in my experience they are usually set just above the level of expected sales.

A final point to watch for. If a publisher's Agreement offers an attractive, extra-high royalty rate – say, 25 or more per cent of list price – then you are probably in danger of getting into bed with a Vanity Publisher (*see* Chapter 10). Get out, quick.

**When are royalties paid?**

Royalties are paid on the basis of copies sold. They are, therefore, paid out when the book is selling. But first, the advance (*see* below) has to be 'earned out'; many authors are never actually paid any royalties on their books.

Publishers keep account of the number of copies of each of their books that are sold; they report sales of their books to each author at regular intervals. Most publishers now report sales at six-monthly intervals: a few continue the older practice of accounting at yearly intervals; a very few, report and account for sales on a monthly basis for the first few months after publication.

The fairly standard six-monthly sales figures are usually reported, and any royalties paid, three months after the period to which they refer. The accounting process takes this long. Publishers work to their own accounting years; there are no standard dates. (For example, Allison & Busby produce sales figures twice yearly, for the periods ending 30 March and 30 September; royalty payments are made in June and December.)

The book-selling industry provides for bookshops to return unsold copies of a book to the publisher. In their Agreements with authors therefore, most publishers now hold back part of the payment of early royalties in case there are significant returns. Between 15 and 25 per cent of royalties earned during the first six-monthly accounting period is often held back – 'retained' – for the period agreed in the contract.

**Why are some overseas sales paid at a lower royalty rate?**

If the royalty is based on UK list price, this is because the publisher gets less money from overseas sales: he has to pay a distributor in the other country and for overseas transport of the books. But it is now more usual for the royalties on overseas sales to be based on a percentage (around 10 per cent) of the publisher's net receipts – just as for big-discount chain-store sales.

# AGENTS, AGREEMENTS AND ADVANCES

## What is, and when do I get, an advance?

As already mentioned, royalties are paid on the basis of sold copies of a book. But the author will have finished virtually all work on the book well before publication. An advance provides the author with payment closer to the work-time.

An advance is just what it says it is: an *advance* payment against expected future earnings. Most Agreements provide for the payment of such an advance. Effectively, there will be only one advance in respect of any one book – but it is frequently paid in instalments. There are three possible times for portions of the advance to be paid:

- on signature of the Agreement,
- on delivery (some Agreements specify 'on acceptance' – which condition should be avoided if possible) of the complete book manuscript,
- on publication of the book.

Different publishers, different agents, different authors, different books can have different payment occasions or numbers of advance portions. Experienced authors' books might attract 50, 25, 25 per cent portions of the advance while first-timers with the same publisher might be offered 25, 25, 50 per cent portions; others may be offered 33, 33, 34 per cent.

Allison & Busby non-fiction book contracts usually allow for 50 per cent on signature and 50 per cent on publication. Another publisher I have worked with pays 50 per cent on delivery and 50 per cent on publication.

Very occasionally, the advance might be a single payment on signature – but I've never yet been that lucky.

## Is the advance in addition to the royalties?

As already explained above, the total advance is a payment in advance of expected future royalty earnings. The author will receive regular statements, but no further royalty payments until the royalties earned, less the proportion withheld against possible booksellers' returns, exceed the amount of the advance – that is, until the advance is 'earned out'.


**Do I have to return the advance if for some reason my book is not published? What if I fail to deliver the manuscript on time? Or suppose the commissioned manuscript is judged unacceptable?**

Generally speaking, any advance already received is non-returnable. Conceivably, a publisher may abandon plans for a new or expanded list after commissioning a book from an author, and signing an Agreement. Or the publisher could cease trading. In such circumstances, no publisher would expect to reclaim the advance. Reputable publishers would pay the remaining portions of an agreed advance.

This happened to me: I signed an Agreement for a book and received the first portion of the advance; the publisher changed owners and dropped the list – and my book, just as I was about to deliver; I was paid the whole of the remaining portion of the advance. And some while later I sold the book to another publisher – earning another advance.

If you are unlikely to be able to deliver a book manuscript by the date specified in the Agreement, you should certainly advise the publisher in advance. Most publishers will take late delivery on board and re-schedule publication. The remainder of the advance would then be paid at the relevant stages. If an author totally fails to deliver a manuscript then the publisher COULD claim back the part of the advance already paid – the Agreement has been broken. Some publishers, however would merely write off the debt.

Publisher and author will usually have entered into an Agreement on the basis of the author's sample chapters; the publisher knows the quality of work the author will produce. There should seldom if ever therefore be any question of a delivered commissioned manuscript being judged 'unacceptable'. Of course, it is not unusual for a publisher of (usually) a non-fiction book to require limited amounts of rewriting to clarify the delivered book text. But there should not usually be any question of the next portion of the advance not being paid. As far as possible, watch out for and avoid 'acceptable manuscript' clauses in your Agreement.

I suppose it is possible that having signed an Agreement, an author might deliver an absolutely rotten book – badly written and totally out of line with the initial submission on which the Agreement was based. In such circumstances the publisher could well decline to publish the book – or to pay the balance of the advance. But they still might well write off the already-paid portions of the advance.

**What if the royalties earned by my book do not amount to as much as the total advance: do I have to repay the difference?**

No. Advances are non-returnable. And it is not at all uncommon for advances – particularly the huge ones occasionally offered to big names – not to be 'earned out'.

**How much should my advance be – on what basis is the size of an advance calculated?**

This is a 'how long is a piece of string' question. A publisher may offer as much – or as little – as is needed to ensure that the author allows him to publish his/her book.

A publishing house will sometimes be keen to have a bestselling author or major new book in its list – and will pay a large advance for the privilege. The size of the advance is a major factor in the auctions of bestsellers' new books. A top author may contemplate moving to a different publisher if a significantly higher advance is offered. Against that, some authors, e.g., those employed in academia, where publication adds kudos and may improve advancement chances, may need little persuasion and will be offered a small advance. A first time author is a greater financial risk to the publisher than an established author: they would usually be offered a smaller advance, reflecting that risk.

But most writers are not (yet) at the top of the heap and cannot hope for news-worthy six-figure advances. There is a rule of thumb by which, in the past, advances were often determined; it is still a useful calculation to get into the right ball park. The advance is calculated as 50 per cent of the royalties that would be earned from the sale of the whole of the book's initial print run.

Thus, assuming a book with a list price of £10, an 8 per cent royalty rate and an estimated (and realistic) first print run of, say 2,000 copies, the advance might be:

2,000 (print run) x £10 (price) x 0.08 (royalty) x 0.5 (half) = £800 (advance)

Authors being offered more than that might think themselves lucky; if offered less, unlucky (or maybe the book is too specialised and lower sales are expected).

Beginners may think that the size of the advance is not particularly important – a small advance merely means that future payments of royalties will be that much greater. But this is not a good way of thinking. A larger advance has two big advantages:

• the publisher will probably work harder to sell a book in which he has invested more money;
• the author has a guaranteed lump sum payment to compensate for all the hard work that has gone into the book – and advances are not always 'earned out'.

**I have had a book published. Before the publisher took it on, I signed two copies of an Agreement and returned them to the publisher. I have not had my copy of the Agreement back – nor have I received any money. The book is getting excellent reviews and the publisher has asked me to write another book. What should I do?**

Assuming that the Agreement you signed was a reasonable one – and you should have sorted that out at that time – you should have received your copy back. I would, long ago, have phoned the publisher for its return: I suggest you do so – NOW. If the Agreement provided for you to be paid an advance – and you would remember that from when you signed it – you should have been paid. When you phone the publisher, enquire whether you should have sent him an invoice for the advance payment(s). This is not usual, but does sometimes apply – and it offers him an excuse.

Some publishers are slow in making payments – they just don't like signing cheques – and may need chasing. If your Agreement did not provide for any advance against royalty earnings, though – and this is sometimes the case with small, particularly non-fiction, books – you may not yet be due for any payment. Your first accounting of sales and payment of earnings could be as much as fifteen months after publication. (Annual accounting, start of year coinciding with publication date, and the usual three months for accounting purposes.)

The book seems to be doing well, the publisher seems happy; you need that Agreement back – it will tell you what you are to be paid and when. Insist on its return – phone them DAILY until you get it back. Then read it carefully to remind yourself what is due. If you should have been paid, phone them and ask what's happened. And if you still get no joy, and no money, get in touch with The Society of Authors (*see* Chapter 2).

**Never leave a business/contractual/financial matter unresolved.**

When you get it all sorted out – and the money flowing satisfactorily – and you are once again happy with the publisher, who still wants another book – go for it.

### Recommended further reading

*The Business of Writing*, Gordon Wells
    (Allison & Busby, London, 1998.)
*Be a Successful Writer: 99 Surefire Checklists*, Gordon Wells
    (Allison & Busby, London, 1999.)

# 8

# DEALING WITH EDITORS

**Has a magazine editor 'the right' to change my work – should I permit this?**

There are various ways of looking at this. An editor's job is to edit. We are all liable to make mistakes or leave something unfinished or unexplained. An editor will always, and rightly, correct such matters and personally, I have never been other than grateful.

There is also a matter of what is known as 'house style'. Some magazines adopt their own style – covering punctuation perhaps, and a preferred choice of alternative spellings. Editors will always make such changes to your work – to maintain the same style throughout their publication. For instance, readers would not wish to see a magazine spelling, say, apologize on one page and apologise on another: *The Oxford Writers' Dictionary* says you should use IZE; the spell checker on my Word97 word processor says it should be ISE. A magazine will prefer consistency above all.

Similarly, a magazine which is laid out in narrow columns will usually prefer shorter paragraphs than one laid out in half-page-wide columns. A 60-word paragraph in a 40 mm wide column would occupy something like 40 column-millimetres; the same paragraph in a magazine using wider columns would appear very short – in a 19 cm wide column, 60 words in a slightly larger font, take up barely 22 column-millimetres. An editor will want his pages to *look* right. He may therefore sub-divide your paras, or cobble appropriate ones together.

Some writers too are prone to waffling: an editor will usually trim away some of this fat – particularly if he needs to make space, for a bigger heading, an illustration or an advertisement. Advertisements are always important: they provide the money that pays for the editorial content.

No editor will deliberately change the sense of what you are saying. If he/she dislikes or disagrees with what you are writing, it's easier simply to reject your work. There's plenty more where that came from. As long as the resultant printed text still makes sense, I don't really mind what an editor does to my work once he's agreed to pay for it. And frequently, editorial changes are for the better. Most editors are good at their job.

Titles are particularly prone to editorial amendment. I guess that about half my articles are retitled by the editor. And I willingly admit that many of the new titles are better than mine.

The formal answer to the question is therefore tricky: your work as submitted, is yours and yours alone. In theory, an editor does not have the right to alter it – but in practice often will, and very seldom to the detriment of the work. An editor's job is to edit – as he/she thinks fit. If you were foolish enough to add a qualification to your submitted work – article or short story – to the effect that it was not to be altered in any way, I feel sure that it would instantly be rejected, without further consideration. Professional writers accept that their work will be edited.

## Will I be consulted about any changes an editor makes to my work?

It would be most unusual for the editor of a popular magazine to go back to a writer for approval of editorial changes. There is seldom time for such consultation. And, it is worth remembering, magazines are ephemeral publications; they are not printed on tablets of stone and few are preserved. In any case, as suggested above, few editorial changes are of great significance – mostly they will preserve the writer's ideas and sense, while frequently enhancing readability and understanding.

The editors of some more prestigious, literary, or academic journals – or more ordinary magazines with long lead times – may sometimes send an edited copy of an accepted piece of work back to the writer for approval. In fifty years of writing for magazines I can only recall being given this opportunity once. So don't hold your breath.

But magazines are not the only media for the publication of a writer's work. Much writing is published in book form – and here the situation differs. There are two levels of book editing: that done by the commissioning editor and the subsequent line- or copy-editing. And, just to make things confusing, these two editors are often one and the same person – wearing different hats, possibly simultaneously.

When you deliver a book manuscript to a publisher it will, once accepted, be edited in great detail by the commissioning editor. This is a *quality* check: designed to ensure that it will be a really good book. Inconsistencies and illogicalities will be noticed and queried; where (non-fiction) explanations are insufficiently clear, you may be asked to rewrite – or approve an editor's own rewrite; where the plot of your novel 'sags' a little, you may be offered suggestions for improvement.

In the world of book publishing it would be highly unusual for *significant* editorial changes to be made and the edited manuscript NOT be referred back to the writer/author for approval. But although they should be, copy-editing changes – punctuation, spelling, minor grammatical changes, which are spotted later in the process – may not always be referred back to the author.

It is possible for an author to rectify over-enthusiastic copy-editing – which does happen – when the page proofs of the book are received, for checking. Care must be taken at proof stage though, to avoid incurring excessive correction costs. Proofs are for correcting, not for rewriting.

**I am writing a series of specialist articles for a non-specialist, general-interest magazine. The editor has once or twice made significant changes to my text making the content inaccurate and the advice inappropriate. This is potentially damaging to my reputation as an expert in this field. What should I do?**

This problem is clearly caused by you not seeing the edited typescript before it goes to press – and as mentioned above, because of time constraints, you are not likely to get to see it. Equally, you don't want this situation to continue: your expert reputation is most important – both to you and to the magazine.

Assuming that you are not being over-pedantic, nor making a fuss over nothing – well, you wouldn't, would you? – you should contact the editor immediately and point out the potential damage that his (or an assistant's) inappropriate editing may cause. No sensible editor wants his readers to be given wrong or misleading advice. It will almost certainly just be a case of lack of understanding of the subtleties involved. You may be able to negotiate for a faxed copy of the edited text to be sent you, if you will agree to turn it round within an hour or so.

But if you *don't* speak to the editor, he'll never know – and could repeat the mistake. Don't worry: although all magazine editors are rushed off their feet, few have been known to bite. The editor *wants* your articles to advise the readers well – not mislead them.

If, after trying, you get nowhere with the editor, I suggest you look elsewhere for a home for your specialist advice.

**The editor of a new magazine has written to me accepting an article idea I offered him. He has addressed the letter to me by my first name (only) – 'Dear John'. How should I reply to him – first name only, or what?**

A large part of the publishing world – magazines and books – communicates on first name terms. Unless and until you have actually got to know this editor, though – have met in person, or have chatted with them comfortably on the phone – I think I'd play it a bit cautiously.

For now, my advice would be to write back to Mr (or Ms) Bloggs – which can't offend – or 'Dear George Bloggs' – which never *feels* right to me – and sign your own name with both first and last names (i.e., not with initials). If you continue corresponding with the same editor, after two or three exchanges, it will feel more right to address the editor as 'Dear George' and sign it John.

**What is an outline – what should it include?**

Increasingly, magazine editors are asking for preliminary queries, outlining the proposed content of a feature article, before giving even a tentative go-ahead. This, of course, saves them from having to review a large pile of complete but largely inappropriate unsolicited offers; it also saves the freelance writer from abortive working up of an idea which isn't going to appeal to the editor. A preliminary query can also give the editor the opportunity to input his/her own ideas to extend, or re-shape the article before the writer gets to work.

A preliminary query therefore is an outline of the content of a proposed article. Its purpose is to demonstrate to the editor that the eventual article will be 'right' for the magazine and will have sufficient interesting content to make it worth considering.

Generally following this sequence, an article outline should include:

- The suggested title for the article – and, if this is not self-evident, the subject of the article.
- The first couple of paragraphs (the 'hook') – so that the editor can see how you propose instantly to 'grab' the reader. The opening paragraphs also give the editor some idea of your ability to write.
- If it is not now apparent – as it will usually be from title and hook – include a paragraph outlining the purpose of the article. Make sure that you know what the purpose is, yourself. If you don't, you can end up with a 'So what?' article – and they don't sell. (A 'So what' article is my name for one which leaves the reader unsatisfied - neither amused, nor stimulated, nor wiser - leading to a shrugged and disappointed 'so what?' response.)
- A number of 'bullet points' (i.e., like this list) listing the key points that the article will deal with. Keep these points brief but, where appropriate, include specific facts. Don't generalise or be vague. The facts will show the editor that you have/will have done the necessary research and have something positive to offer.
- If the article is to include quotes from specialists or relevant anecdotes, give details of these sources.
- End the outline itself with the 'statistics' – suggested length, proposed number and type of illustrations (colour, black-and-white, line-drawings, etc.), and, if relevant, forthcoming events/anniversaries, etc., to which the feature could be linked and the deadline by which you could supply the finished material. Note that your delivery intentions are of less relevance for non date-related features.

The above – which should be restricted to one sheet of single-spaced typescript – will, hopefully, sell the article idea. All that now remains on the same single sheet of typescript is to sell yourself as the person to write it.

- In no more than about one hundred words, outline your writing credentials and subject-specific expertise. If you have written for a number of magazines (irrespective of subject) mention the best known one or two. If you haven't, don't mention it. Specifically, don't say something like, 'This is my first attempt at writing a feature article …' That's the kiss of death. If you have written books, say so. If you have professional qualifications or personal experience relevant to the article subject, mention these.
- Finally, at the bottom of the single sheet, give your name, address and phone/fax number and, if available, e-mail address.

Send the one-page outline with a brief covering letter – and the inevitable stamped addressed envelope. The covering letter need say little more than:

> Dear Mr Bloggs [always try to address a name]
> I write to enquire if you would be interested in a 000-word [illustrated] article tentatively entitled 'My Article' for publication in your magazine at your normal payment rates. I enclose an outline of the proposed article: I would, within my competence, be willing to adjust the content, proposed length and type of illustrations should you so wish. I also enclose a stamped addressed envelope. I look forward to hearing from you.
> Yours sincerely

And a warning. Despite the inclusion of the stamped addressed envelope, editors do not always reply to article outlines. If they like what you are offering, they'll get in touch – possibly by phone. If not, they may just bin your submission. Sad, but true. The only excuse is that editors are invariably frantically busy.

**Should I send a magazine editor a separate outline, or incorporate the outline in a query letter?**

American advice suggests that some American editors welcome outlines/queries in the form of an inclusive, fairly 'pushy', sales letter. In my experience, British editors are happier with a brief, business-like covering letter and an outline on a separate sheet. Certainly, the separate approach is my own preferred method. Whichever the approach, the content of an article outline or query letter is much the same.

Within the limits imposed by different editorial requirements, style, length and 'slant', it may be possible for an article outline to be used more than once – submitted to different magazines, with a personalised covering letter. Agreed, the same advantage can largely be obtained by judicious 'cut-and-pasting' of the outline 'meat' into individual covering letters.

Where I have worked for a particular magazine and editor several times before, I sometimes vary the above approach and suggest maybe a couple of article ideas within a single letter. In such circumstances, I offer fewer details, merely describing the article content and purpose. This assumes that the editor knows my style and ability to deliver what he/she wants.

Although many editors specify queries (or outlines) only, I will often submit the completed article if it is not more than about 800 words long. There is little more work entailed in completing such shorter pieces than in preparing a good, 'selling' outline.

**Editors often ask for an outline to be accompanied by photocopies of published work of a similar nature. What do I do if I haven't had anything (similar) published before?**

This is the 'chicken-and-egg' scenario. And there's no easy answer. The first point to make though is that there are still many magazines that don't ask to see published work. If you start by writing for those magazines – which are often at either the low-paying or the specialist end of the market – you can build up the portfolio of published work needed to convince the other editors of your ability.

That approach is not always possible though. The other approach is, if you have had anything published anywhere (i.e., nationally – not the parish magazine), on any subject – enclose a photocopy of that.

And if you haven't yet broken your duck – just send in the outline with no accompanying photocopy. If it's really good – and even more important, right for the target magazine – you will sometimes get an invitation to submit on spec.

Then all you have to do is make the completed article as good as the outline suggested – and cross your fingers.

**In response to an outline, what sort of a go-ahead will I get – and having got it, what do I do?**

Many editors, responding to an interesting-looking outline, will ask you to submit the finished article for consideration. This is not a commission, nor is it a contract. You will still be submitting on spec – but you are in with a good chance of acceptance. The editor is interested and hopefully will remember and recognise your submission when it lands on his/her desk. Don't keep the editor waiting too long though or his/her memory will have faded. If you said that you could produce the final article within so many weeks – deliver on time. Earlier is better.

Some magazine editors will write to say go-ahead, specifying length, delivery deadline and offered payment. This is a commission. The letter – unless it specifically makes clear, as above, that it is not a commission, merely a willingness to consider the work on spec – taken with your outline and your eventual delivery of the agreed work, together constitute a contract.

Occasionally, and more usually from the higher-paying and more 'up-market' magazines, you will, on the basis of the outline and your 'credentials', be offered a formal contract to produce the proposed article. This will usually specify such matters as delivery deadline, length, illustrations … and payment details. It *should* also make provision for the payment of a 'kill fee' in respect of possible non-use of the completed work (*see* Chapter 4).

What do you do when you get a go-ahead? Why, go ahead, of course. Deliver what you have offered, within the time you and/or the editor have specified. Make it as good as you possibly can. And always remind the editor of his/her willingness to consider it or his/her commission, quoting dates of relevant correspondence.

**I recently submitted an article outline to an editor. He replied, saying that he already had something similar 'in the pipeline' but would 'keep my details on file'. What does this mean and is it 'a good thing'?**

Broadly speaking, such a comment doesn't mean much. However, if you offered a particularly specialist feature – say, about one narrow field of antique collecting to a generalist collecting magazine – then, 'your details on file' just might lead to a later commission if and when the magazine needs something about your specialist field.

Another meaning, which is just as likely, is that the editor merely wanted to let you down lightly.

It's only 'a good thing' if something comes of it. Don't hold your breath.

# 9

# THE MECHANICS OF SUBMISSION

**How – i.e., in what format – should I submit my work to editors and/or publishers?**

Whether article, short story, novel or non-fiction book, the basic submission format is the same. Your work must be typed, or printed on a word-processor printer, on one side only of white, A4-sized paper of about 80 gsm. I use good quality copier paper.

The text should be double-spaced – that is, a full line space between each line of print – and have wide margins. The margins should be about 40 mm at the top and on the left and about 25 mm at right and bottom. It matters not whether your typewriter has *elite* or *pica* typeface, either is OK. With a word processor printer choose an 'ordinary' font at about 10 to 12-point size. I use 11-point Tahoma, a sans-serif font but Times New Roman or Univers would be equally acceptable. As far as possible, maintain a standard number of lines per page – this makes it easier for an editor to check the length.

Pages should be numbered. My preference is to put this in the top right corner, as part of an identification 'header': a key word from the title, my surname and the page number, but some writers prefer an identification-only header with the page number at the foot of the page. No one's going to be too fussy about this though – just as long as the information's there.

Paragraph-starts should be indented by a consistent amount – 15 mm is usual; but do not indent the first paragraph after a title, chapter title or internal subheading. Do not – as is common business practice – leave a line space between paragraphs; reserve such a line-space:

• to indicate the passage of time or a change of scene or viewpoint in a short story or novel. This space is sometimes decorated with a short, centred line of asterisks.

- for above and below a sub-heading – to separate it from the rest of the text. I use two blank spaces above a heading and one below.
- to separate a list (e.g., of bullet-points like this) or a quotation from the rest of the text.

The title of an article or short story should be centred, in capitals, about half a dozen (double-spaced) lines down the first page, followed, a couple of lines below, by your name (or pen-name – *see* page 25) in lower case text, again, centred. Neither title nor name should be underlined – I usually print title and name in bold. A further couple of lines down start the text (and don't indent the first para).

At the end of an article or short story, type the word END. Beneath this, type your (real, if writing under a pen-name) name and address; I put this in a single line across the page.

Articles and short stories should also have a cover sheet. About a third of the way down an A4 page, give the title (capitals, not underlined, bold if possible, and centred). About four (single-spaced) lines down, type your name/pen-name, also centred. Half a dozen lines further down give the length of the piece – 'Approximately 000 words.' At the left hand bottom corner of the page, in a block, type your (real) name and address and phone/fax number. You may also wish to give an e-mail address.

If the cover sheet is for a short story you should also – I suggest at the top right corner of the page but the location is optional – mention that you are offering First British Serial Rights (show as F.B.S.R. *see* page 61.) This is not normally necessary for an article.

The only differences when preparing a book typescript are that you should give the number and title of each chapter but not your name and should not mark END at the end of each chapter. You should start a fresh page for each new chapter, but the page numbering runs on throughout the book.

For a novel, a title page is all that is required, covering all the pages in the book. This should be much like a short story or article cover page, but with no mention of the rights being offered – you're offering book rights. Give the total book wordage on the title page. For a non-fiction book a full set of *prelims* (preliminary pages) and *end-matter* (including an index) will normally be required.

Presentation of a non-fiction book requires further consideration. *See* my book, *How to Write Non-Fiction Books*.

When submitting a short story or article to a magazine which welcomes unsolicited manuscripts, I include a short, business-like covering letter and – always – a stamped addressed envelope. The covering letter need say little more than:

Dear Mr Bloggs/Joe (always address an editor by name)
I enclose herewith, for your consideration for publication at your usual payment rates (always make it clear that you expect to be paid – some small publications may not pay unless this is made clear) a 000-word article/short story entitled TITLE. (Mention number of photographs enclosed, if relevant.)
I also enclose a stamped addressed envelope for the return of the manuscript if it is not of interest. If accepted, I would appreciate a copy of the issue of MAGAZINE in which it appears. I look forward to hearing from you.
Yours sincerely

If you have already successfully sounded-out the editor with a query letter (*see* page 103), refer to his/her expression of interest when submitting the resultant article or story.

### What is the best way to approach a publisher about my novel or non-fiction book?

With a first novel it would probably be wise to write a letter to a chosen publisher (or to a number of publishers) enquiring whether they would be willing to look at your book. Your letter should describe the book enthusiastically – and suggest that you send them a synopsis plus the first three chapters. And always enclose a stamped addressed envelope.

Many publishers will write back and decline, suggesting that you should get yourself an agent. But some publishers will agree to look at your book – and will probably ask, as suggested, for the synopsis plus three chapters. Deliver these as soon as possible – before they can forget.

It will often be better if you can submit your novel through an agent. (*See* page 86.) But agents can be as hard to get as publishers. It's a hard hard world out there.

It is somewhat easier to approach a publisher about a non-fiction book. Most relevant publishers will be willing to consider a well-thought-out, well presented, non-fiction book proposal.

I recommend submitting a detailed synopsis plus a statement of the proposed book's objectives, its target readership, its competition, and its 'selling points' – why it is needed and why you are the person to write it. Submit a proposal of this type to one or more relevant publishers and, in a brief covering letter, offer to provide a couple of sample chapters and/or to adjust the synopsis should the publisher so wish. If the book is worth publishing and you have selected your target publishers well, you have a reasonable chance of getting a go-ahead.

## YOU SHOULD ALWAYS SELL YOUR NON-FICTION BOOK BEFORE YOU WRITE IT.

### How long do publishers take to respond – to enquiries and/or submissions?

On the whole, book publishers are pretty good about responding to submissions. Certainly they are better than many magazine editors. I would expect a brief letter saying yes or no to a preliminary enquiry about interest in seeing a submission within a few weeks – less than a month. I would expect a response to a fuller submission – synopsis plus sample chapters – within about three months. You will usually get an acknowledgement of receipt by return.

A long delay in responding to a fuller submission could well mean that the publisher is seeking a further reader's opinion to support an initial recommendation. Rejections tend to come more quickly.

If you haven't heard anything after three months, I suggest a polite, businesslike letter enquiring about news – or perhaps a quick phone call. But don't forget, you want them to buy something – they're in the chair.

**Why do I have to send a stamped addressed envelope every time I write to a magazine or publisher?**

Magazines and publishers receive huge piles of unsolicited material daily. Much of it is worthless, or at best, badly targeted. It would be very expensive for them to pay the return postage on everything that they get. So – if you want a reply, send a stamped addressed envelope (s.a.e.). Note: in America they call this an s.a.s.e. – meaning self-addressed stamped envelope.

Once you are accepted, or on reasonable terms with a publisher or an editor, you will often be able to dispense with the s.a.e. Initially though – send one every time. Even with an s.a.e., some magazine editors don't bother to respond to unacceptable ideas or query letters.

**How can I get a commission for a magazine article?**

Two ways. First, if you already well-known to an editor and he/she particularly wants a feature article on a subject relevant to your expertise, the editor may contact you, specify what is required and offer you a commission. Secondly, as a result of a query letter/outline (*see* page 103), you may be lucky enough to get a commission – rather than the more usual, 'We'd like to see this article, but without commitment.'

**Will a magazine editor tell me what he/she thinks of my short story or article – and if not, how can I find out whether or not my work is any good?**

Magazine editors are not in the business of offering criticisms of submitted work. Apart from anything, they're usually too busy. If your work is acceptable, they'll accept it, if not, they'll reject it.

One exception to that comment: the editors at D. C. Thomson magazines are often more helpful than most: if your article or story is 'almost there' they will sometimes make suggestions for improving it – for re-submission. But don't ask for this or assume it – it's just them being helpful.

Very occasionally, an editor rejecting a piece of work will scribble a few helpful words on the cover sheet – if possible, take particular note of such comments and submit something else, soon.

How then can you find out whether or not your work is any good? There are various ways:

- Self-criticism/appraisal – leave your work alone at for three or four weeks (or until it has been rejected and returned) and then re-read it. The delay will enable you to make a more detached, better judgement/criticism.
- Competitions – many competitions, whether small, writers' circle internal competitions, or national magazine competitions, offer the judge's comments on all entries. Winning a competition, however small, can also give your *ego* a boost.
- Critique services – a number of people, many of them well-experienced published writers, offer such services. They advertise regularly in the writing magazines. But their crits are often expensive – you should assess their likely skills before indulging.

    Again, the relatively new and successful agency, Midland Exposure, which has already been mentioned, will look at short stories, for a reading fee of a few pounds. (For details – *see* page 86).
- Writers' circles, workshops and evening classes – most of these will offer criticism of members' work. But the value of the criticism depends on the expertise or knowledge of the person offering it. Beware the blind leading the blind and take amateur criticism with a pinch or ten of salt.


**How soon after I submit a short story or article to a magazine should I expect a response?**

Most magazines will respond with a decision within about four to six weeks. Some take much longer. If you haven't heard after about six weeks it is usually worth a quick, businesslike phone call to the relevant – fiction or features – editor asking when a response can be expected. A word of caution though: at least one magazine editor warns that over-diligent enquiries in less than three months cause instant rejection. As you work with magazines you will soon get to know which ones are quick and which slow, which ones to 'chase' and which not. But always remember that you are operating in a buyer's market.

### Should I send an invoice with an on spec submission of a short story or article?

Mostly, no, except with commissioned work for which a fee has been agreed. With on spec submissions, it is best to wait for the editor to ask for an invoice if one is required.

However, if a piece of work is accepted and published and payment appears to be slow in coming, it is worth checking whether or not they require an invoice and forgot to tell you. It is often best to phone the magazine's accounts department, and ask them whether they need an invoice. You don't have to bother the editor.

Anyway, after the first submission, you will soon get to know which magazines require invoices and which don't. If you need to provide an invoice but – as is often the case – don't know how much you will be paid, submit the invoice with the amount left blank. The editor will fill in the gap.

### Can I submit my articles or short stories to more than one magazine at a time?

NO. That's a real, definite, absolute no-no. Whether specified (as with a short story) or not (as with an article), you are offering a magazine First British (or other) Serial Rights. If two editors pick up your offer, who is first? And if both magazines were to publish the work simultaneously both editors would, rightly, be hopping mad. Your name would be blacklisted around the profession.

### Can I submit a book idea or manuscript to more than one publisher at a time?

Some years ago, it was considered most improper to submit a book idea or manuscript to more than one publisher at a time – and if they didn't reject the idea almost immediately, they each took two or three months to consider it. Nowadays though, publishers are more accustomed to the idea of multiple submissions.

In fairness to the publishers, they should always be told when a book proposal or manuscript is being offered to other publishers at the same time – but it is not necessary to tell them WHICH other publishers.

So – you CAN. But SHOULD you? I think that a beginning author offering a first novel themselves would be wisest to submit to only one carefully chosen publisher. But maybe I'm being over-cautious/old-fashioned. If the first novel is being handled by an agent, the agent may well offer to more than one publisher at a time – but that is for the agent to decide. After the first novel, multiple submissions by the author are more realistic. Book 'auctions' – as for best-selling blockbusters – inevitably involve multiple submissions and a bidding process; such things are best left to agents to arrange and negotiate. Don't try doing it on your own.

An experienced non-fiction writer might well offer a book proposal – synopsis plus statement of objectives, etc. – to two or three carefully selected publishers at the same time. And, because at this stage with a non-fiction book the author is seeking a go-ahead and contract for a still-to-be-written book, once any publisher shows real interest, the others should be advised. But in many cases there is just one preferred/most likely publisher and a unique submission direct to that pub-lisher would therefore be best.

### Should I use a word processor?

There is no doubt that, once you have got past the initial learning stage, a word processor is the most wondrous thing any writer could possess:

- you type at a (more-or-less) conventional keyboard;
- your words appear on screen before you – and *what you see is what you get*;
- you can correct as you go – spelling errors are highlighted and corrections offered;
- you can move whole sections of writing about within a story or article – you can change anything almost instantaneously;
- and you can print out a 'hard' copy as and when you want.

Word processors used to be expensive; nowadays, they're cheap. A PC (personal computer) – which will not merely process words but also keep business accounts, access and/or store vast amounts of information and even let you play games when you're 'blocked' (*see* page 81) – now costs little more than an electronic typewriter did a few years ago. A writer doesn't need a computer with all the latest bells and whistles on it; an outdated model being sold off cheap will almost certainly be ideal. Then you're in business.

To be strictly accurate, the word processor is the program that tells the PC what to do. There have been many word processor programs available over the years and they've steadily got better. Today, it doesn't really matter which word processor program you choose, they are nearly all compatible with each other. The world's most-used word processor program of all though is almost certainly Microsoft's WORD. It will do everything you could possibly need – apart from coming up with fresh ideas or storylines.

There's no compulsion to use a word processor – but if you don't, you're missing out. Get one if you possibly can.

**What sort of printer should I use with my word processor?**

The choice, nowadays, is between an ink-jet printer or a laser printer. Both produce work of excellent appearance – the characters and lines are slightly finer with a laser printer but these tend to cost more than ink-jets. Against that, the operating costs of a laser printer are usually less than those for an ink-jet.

At present there are plenty of ink-jet printers on sale at around £100; the cheapest laser printer is nearer £200. I use an ink-jet printer myself but am frequently tempted to buy a laser one. The choice is yours.

**Does it matter which typeface/font (on my word processor printer) I use for my manuscripts?**

No – as long as it's an 'ordinary' one. Avoid mock handwriting or similar fonts – go for something like Tahoma (my current favourite), or Univers, or Times New

Roman. Standardise on one font and use it for just about all your writing work. For manuscripts use a font-size of about 10- to 12-point. (I use 11-point Tahoma.)

**Why is the layout of my work so important – after all, it's going to be converted into magazine or book pages?**

You know what they say, 'You only get one chance to make a first impression.' Your typescript is effectively your shop-window. If it looks good, you're over the first hurdle – after that it's what you write that will count.

Professionals present their work well. Their layout is professional-looking. Badly presented work looks amateurish. That puts you one down before you start.

**There are some corrected typing errors (typos) in my manuscript. Does this matter? How many typos are 'permissible'?**

If you are still using a 'steam' typewriter, I suppose you would be 'excused' the odd one or two corrections per A4 page. (But do save up for a word processor.)

If you are using a word processor, there shouldn't be ANY significant errors/corrections in your submitted copy. Rather than correct in ink, correct on screen and reprint relevant pages. It takes no time at all.

Always check your work before you send it out. We're back to layout and presentation again – and looking professional.

**Physically, how should I bundle and pack up a synopsis and three sample chapters to send to a publisher?**

With the chapters double-spaced and the synopsis probably single-spaced, this bundle is going to amount to maybe 60 pages of A4. Together with this you will need to send a covering letter and an adequately-sized reply-paid envelope – and possibly a small s.a.e. too, for an acknowledgement. You might wish to paperclip each of the book's chapters separately – I suggest not. I would, though, staple the pages of the synopsis together to keep it separate from the text proper. Fold the reply envelope once, so that it is smaller than an A4 sheet. Stretch an elastic band around the whole bundle. You may consider including an A4-sized sheet of thin card to stiffen the package but with 60-plus sheets this is not really necessary.

You may feel that ordinary brown Manilla C4-sized envelopes (324 x 229 mm, i.e., to take A4 contents) are perhaps not strong enough to protect your 'baby'. You could cross-tape two ways around the envelope with transparent sticky tape – just don't make it impossible to open at the publishers.

The alternatives are to buy some of the much stronger 'tear-proof' Tyvek envelopes – but unfortunately these only come in packs of 25 costing several pounds, which are fine if you use a lot, as I do – or a Jiffy or Mail-Lite padded envelope, which can usually be bought one at a time.

If you despatch your material to a publisher in a padded envelope – and want it to be similarly returned – then a reply-paid envelope is a problem. Padded envelopes don't fold. In this situation, I would recommend enclosing a sufficiently stamped and self-addressed sticky label.


**I have sold three feature articles to a 'quality' magazine – and been well paid for them. But that was two years ago and the articles still haven't been published. I am eager to see my articles in print – and to be able to show them to other editors. What can I do?**


Two years is quite a long time to wait. And I can understand your frustration. There isn't a great deal you can do about this situation, though – they have purchased your work, it is for them to decide when to use it. But some suggestions.

The magazine sounds like a good market: they paid well and on acceptance. I would be offering them more work … all the time. Submitting further work to them would refresh your name in the editor's memory. And in my covering letters, I would occasionally remind them of the material they have bought and not yet used.

If you can't think of a suitable new idea to offer them, you could try writing them a polite letter enquiring about when they might be using your articles. There's always a chance that the articles might just have been overlooked/forgotten. Ensure that any enquiry is polite and businesslike though; if you're too 'stroppy' you may close off your future chances in this potentially good market.

# 10

# MAKING A BOOK OF IT

## How well does the 'average book' sell?

Because there's no such thing as an 'average book', this is an impossible question to answer. But here are a few yardsticks.

A typical first, 'straight' or literary, novel – with nothing particular going for it, other than one editor's instinct – coming out in hardback only, might sell little more than one thousand copies. A similar novel written in one of the popular *genres* might get up to two thousand copies. But that would need luck.

If either of those novels proved a success in hardback and went into a (mass market) paperback edition, sales could easily rise into the five figure bracket. Many first novels however, never make the step from hardback to paperback.

At the other end of the scale, a 'heavyweight' Booker Prize winner – i.e., a literary novel – can achieve six-figure sales. Arundhati Roy's *God of Small Things* sold just under 600,000 copies in 1998 alone. But that is, so far, a record. In *genre* fiction, a handful of really big names – John Grisham, Catherine Cookson, Patricia Cornwell, Dick Francis, etc. – regularly notch up paperback sales of around half a million copies in their first year in print.

And the bestselling book of all time is, of course, non-fiction – *The Bible*.

Coming back down to earth – with a bump – a run-of-the-mill non-fiction book, published in trade paperback (the format in which this book is produced) might sell two or three thousand copies.

As another example, my own *The Craft of Writing Articles* in this series has been around since 1983 and gone through several printings of the two editions. So far, it has achieved sales of just over 17,000. In its own context, this would class as a bestseller.

Sticking my neck out, if you sell, say, 5,000 copies of any book (other than a mass-market paperback), you are not doing at all badly – 2,000 is much more usual.

### How many copies of a book are published in a first edition?

Another 'how long is a piece of string' question. And the 'piece of string' is getting shorter with each new technological development. It is now possible – but not yet commonplace – for a publisher to print on demand. A first edition could therefore be no more than enough to satisfy immediate requirements – review copies, library copies, and a few samples for bookshops. At present though, publishers still print a sizeable initial run.

A first print run for a hardback novel could well be no more than 1,000 copies, 2,000 copies would usually be the limit. The first print run of a mass market paperback novel might be 10,000 copies. The first print run of a trade paperback might be as high as 1,000 but is now often less.

Economics is still a factor in the size of the initial print run: as the run increases, the unit cost drops – but no publisher wants a stack of left-over books not selling at all. The publisher has to strike a balance between print run and unit cost.

But the question was actually about the size of the first edition. In a single edition, there will be virtually no changes in the text, other than minor typographical corrections; significant textual changes would be classed as a fresh edition. There can be any number of print runs or *impressions* or reprints within a single edition. Clearly, it is even more difficult to put a print-run figure to a whole first edition.

### What is a trade paperback?

The distinction between mass market and trade paperback is blurring. Nevertheless, trade paperbacks are still different: they are produced in far smaller numbers than their mass market cousins; they usually have a slightly bigger page size, they may be printed on a better quality paper – and because of their smaller print run, they cost more (but less than a hardback).

Many books – like this one – are produced directly in trade paperback, omitting hardback publication and with little or no expectation of going into mass market. It represents, of course, a publisher's assessment of likely sales potential.

**What does a new edition entail for an author?**

For a novelist, nothing – unless there were mistakes in the first edition that have to be corrected. A new edition of a novel will often be no more than publication in a different format – hardback into paperback, etc.

For a non-fiction author, though, a new edition has to be brought up to date. If the non-fiction book is a biography or popular history book, this will seldom entail many changes; if it is a how-to or other instructional book there may be a lot to be done.

When you write a non-fiction how-to book, you are expected to keep yourself up-to-date in that field. When the first edition of a book is nearly sold out, or has been around for rather a long time, the publisher may approach the author to update the book. Provision for such up-dating is usually included in the Agreement for a how-to book. The alternative is for the publisher to find another expert to update your book – the cost of which updating will be a first charge on the author's future royalties.

A second edition may be as much as a (non-specific), say, fifty per cent rewrite or a mere up-dating of dated statistics and addresses. A second edition should though, still be recognisably the same book as the first edition: if you're going to rewrite the lot, make it a new book.

**How do I identify/find the 'right' publisher for my book?**

There are hundreds of publishers in Britain. They vary from the huge international firms publishing hundreds of new titles each year to the small independent, often virtually one-person businesses, issuing a mere handful of cherished books annually. And every publishing house has its own unique character, its particular interests, its method of operating. It is the task of the budding author – and/or the agent representing the author – to find the most suitable publisher for his/her book.

There are several ways – applicable to both fiction and non-fiction books – to *start* the process of finding the 'right' publisher:

- Look at the books on your own shelves. Because those books reflect your own tastes, your own book is likely to be fairly similar to some of them – take note of the publishers.
- Browse around the shelves of bookshops and your local library. Look for books like yours – and note the publishers.
- Consult the latest available Spring or Autumn Books special edition of *The Bookseller* – the weekly magazine of the book trade. This will list most of the new books to be published by many (but, unfortunately, not all) of the leading UK publishers in the following six months. Novels are listed by *genre*, non-fiction by subjects; and most of the publishers also advertise their books in the same issue. This issue of *The Bookseller* should be available in your local library – or talk nicely, in a slack business moment, to a friendly bookshop manager. Again, look for relevant and interesting-looking publishers and take notes.
- With or without the above notes, consult one or more of the usual writers' reference books:

  > *Writers & Artists Yearbook* (A. & C. Black, London, annually)
  > *The Writer's Handbook*, edited by Barry Turner (Macmillan, London, annually)
  > *The Guide to Book Publishers* (Writers' Bookshop, Peterborough, UK, annually) This contains details of many more of the smaller publishers than do the other two.

From all the above, make a list of your 'preferred' publishers. Do not concentrate too much of your selection on the big name publishers – you may do just as well, and get much more personal treatment, with one of the smaller firms.

Contact the publishers on your list and ask each for a copy of their current catalogue. Browse carefully through them. You should now be able to arrange your initial list of 'preferred' publishers in some sort of ranking.

Now you can start approaching the publishers with or about your work.

**Is there any scope for getting poetry published?**

Brutally, not a lot. A handful of mainstream publishers publish a handful of books of poetry a year. You have to be extremely good, well-known and lucky, for your collection of poems to be accepted by them. There are also a number of independent, small press publishers of poetry books – but it's no good expecting to make much in the way of royalties from them. The public – including poets themselves – buy few books of poetry.

Few mainstream magazines publish much poetry – and what little they do publish is lowly paid. There are dozens of independent, small press magazines which publish poetry. Most don't pay at all.

But don't give up hope altogether. Poetry is particularly suitable for self-publication. I strongly recommend *How to Publish Your Poetry* by Peter Finch (Allison & Busby, London, 1985 and completely revised in 1998). Peter is a fine poet and author: he has been conventionally published and self-published. He has also been a bookseller. Whatever you need to know about publishing poetry he's been there, done it, and probably designed the T-shirt to go with it. He suggests a print run of no more than 300 copies for a self-published book of poetry.

Poets should also take particular note of the numerous poetry competitions around. Many of these offer sizeable prize-money. Many include publication of winning entries. Be careful though, of competitions with large entry fees, that provide for publication of virtually every entry. Some of these are dubious. If taken to extremes, the poet could be paying (excessively) for the publication of his/her work. This may be vanity publishing – *see* below.

**Who designs book covers – does the author have any say?**

The design of a book cover is the responsibility of the publisher. The cover of any book is an important factor in selling the book. And publishers know what sort of cover will boost sales, and which will not. It's their job. Remember that what's good for the publisher, i.e., better sales, is good for you too.

The publisher will usually engage a specialist freelance artist for the cover. The artist will probably skim through the book to get a feel for what is required. Or he may get a detailed brief from the publisher.

Some publishers send an author a proof of their cover and will consider comments – retaining the final say. Virtually all publishers will send the author an advance copy of their book cover – frequently though, too late for the author's comments to be taken into account. If there is something really wrong, of course, changes will be made. My name was incorrect on the advance publicity cover of one of my books: initials – and wrong – instead of my first name. That was changed.

Very occasionally, and then usually only with the smaller publishers of non-fiction books, the author will be invited to offer suggestions for the cover design.

I was lucky in being allowed to help with the design of the covers for two of my engineering textbooks. My design ideas certainly did no harm to the sales – and both covers still look pretty good to me.

At the other extreme, some publishers buy up ready-made illustrations, previously used in magazine stories, for their paperback books. Much as it undoubtedly grieves the author, no one else is going to be too worried if the girl in the loving clinch on the cover has different coloured hair to the girl in the story.

**I saw an advertisement from a publisher, inviting submissions, and sent them my 100,000-word novel. They say that they are interested in publishing it but need me to make a sizeable contribution towards the cost. Their terms look reasonable, though, and they offer attractive royalty rates. What should I do?**

Run like mad. Get away quick. This is shark-infested water – and you're the dish of the day.

Reputable mainstream publishers NEVER advertise for submissions – they always have far more than they can cope with. And other than in exceptional circumstances, *see* below, no reputable publisher will ask for any payment at all. They pay you.

You have fallen for the wiles of a typical vanity publisher. They tell virtually everyone that their work is good and publishable. The 'contribution' they are asking you to make will cover all of their expenses and provide them with a handsome profit to boot.

Should you sign their contract they will do little or no editing of your book; they will set it up in print and produce possibly only a small number of bound copies, a few of which they will deliver to you, the proud 'parent'. They will undoubtedly 'register' the book – they have to, and it doesn't cost them anything. They may even do a little advertising – but few, if any, booksellers will take copies of the book to sell, because they recognise the name of the publisher and know that their publications are worthless. The vanity publisher's commitment to high royalty rates means nothing when the sales are non-existent.

Vanity publishers are so called because they will 'publish' anything as long as you are paying; they are pandering to the foolish author's vanity. If you cannot find a mainstream publisher to publish your work (and pay you) then you could achieve the same sop to your vanity – but at less cost – by self-publishing. *See* below.

Earlier in this answer I mentioned that, in exceptional circumstances, a reputable mainstream publisher might look for a financial contribution towards the cost of publication. This could be, for example, in the case of a history of a commercial firm or large organisation, where copies of the book are likely to sell only to a restricted and associated audience. A publisher might persuade the firm or organisation to contribute towards the cost in order to make the book financially viable and the firm or organisation might be willing to do so in order to keep the price down and thereby facilitate its purchase by employees, etc.

**I have approached a number of publishers about my book but no one is prepared to publish it. Yet I am convinced that it is a good book and *deserves* to be published. Should I – indeed, can I – publish it myself?**

Generally speaking, if a book is worth publishing – AND IF THERE IS A MARKET FOR IT – then there ought to be a publisher willing to publish it conventionally. The qualification is particularly important. Publishers are in business to make money. If your book will make money for them, someone will pick it up: if it won't make money for a publisher, it probably won't make money for a self-publisher either.

If I were to write a really marvellous how-to book about collecting dustbin lids, it would not find a publisher for the simple reason that only thee and me are mad enough to collect dustbin lids. Projected sales of just two copies is hardly a good proposition.

There are exceptions to the above 'rule'. The history of a village or local stately home could have reasonable sales prospects within the narrow local area. A mainstream publisher would probably not wish to take on such a confined market whereas a self-published book might well be worthwhile. Similarly, if you are an expert in a particularly specialised field and know the specialist market-place, then a self-published book on that specialism could be a practical proposition.

I know an expert in one of the martial arts which has it's own specialist magazine. He has self-published a how-to book and sells it successfully through the specialist magazine and at his own instruction classes. Another acquaintance is an expert on home swimming pools: his self-published book is a recognised authority. It is advertised in specialist magazines and sells well at a high price per copy. Neither of these books would be attractive to a mainstream publisher dealing with mainstream bookshops nation-wide.

As already mentioned above, poetry too is potentially a good case for self-publishing.

Novels, on the other hand, are seldom sensible choices for self-publishing. But there have of course been notable exceptions to that judgement: author Jill Paton Walsh, for instance, effectively self-published her *Knowledge of Angels* which was then shortlisted for the 1994 Booker Prize.

With a growing number of printing firms offering ever-improving facilities for short print runs, though, more and more novels are being self-published. And some authors are moving onto the Internet to publish their fiction. But that is still a new and relatively untried market. Overall though, at least so far, really successful self-published novels are few and far between.

And self-publishing your autobiography/memoirs is – except as a family record – an even bigger no-no.

*Can* you self-publish your book? Certainly – but bear in mind the caveats above. Before you proceed though, consider what self-publishing entails. I go into this in more detail in the next answer but for now, think about the capital cost of producing the book and the considerable time you will need to devote to the selling process. If you think of yourself as a writer you may not enjoy the essential entrepreneurial tasks involved. Or vice versa.

**What does self-publishing entail?**

The first myth to demolish is that of Desk-top Publishing (DTP). Computer programs with such titles are misnomers. The most such programs will do is prepare camera-ready copies of your book's pages. This is no more than the equivalent of the layout and typesetting processes.

To self-publish your book you will need to:

- write the book;
- decide that it warrants publication – i.e., make an unbiased judgement of your own work;
- finance the entire publication process;
- edit your own text – or pay a professional editor to edit it for you;
- design and typeset the pages of the book – or pay a professional to do this for you;
- design the cover, including arranging for the artwork and writing the blurb;
- negotiate with printers and book-binders for the printing and binding of the book;
- arrange for the marketing of the book – which includes advertising, PR (reviews, etc.), selling (usually on sale or return terms) and delivering to bookshops, direct selling, packing and despatch of mail-ordered books … and so on.

All that is a lot of non-writing entrepreneurial work. Be sure you're up to it.

For further wise and detailed advice on self-publishing there is no better book available than Peter Finch's *How To Publish Yourself* (*see* below). As mentioned above, in the context of publishing poetry, Peter has done it all. And survived.

If you decide to self-publish it will also be well worth your while to contact, and join, the helpful, non-profit-making Author-Publisher Network, founded some years ago by the successful self-publisher, John Dawes. Details of the Network from SKS, St. Aldhelm, 20 Paul Street, Frome, Somerset BA11 1DX.

**I have self-published my novel – with some success. I have sold more than three quarters of the first, small, print run and broken even. Recently, book-shops have asked about 'remaindered copies'. What does this mean and what effect or impact will it have on my book?**

First, congratulations: a) on your good sense in only having a small print run, and b) on your book selling so well, and c) on breaking even financially. You've done much better than most.

Now the question. When a book published by a mainstream publisher has 'run out of steam' and copies are no longer shifting out of the warehouse, they are sometimes considered not to be earning their shelf-space. To clear the space, a finance-oriented publisher may decide to sell these books off at a reduced price.

There are specialist dealers who will buy such 'dead stock' books – known as remaindered copies – at a much reduced price. The publishers usually sell them for about ten per cent of the published price. Mainstream publishers should offer such books first to the author – at the remainder price. Individual bookshops buy these remaindered books, from the specialist dealers, to offer as 'Bargain Books'. And there are at least two firms specialising in selling remaindered books to the public:

• Bibliophile, 5 Thomas Road, London E14 7BN (Tel: 020 7515 9222)
• Postscript, 24 Langroyd Road, London SW17 7PL (Tel: 020 8767 7421)

They are worth remembering when you are looking for books about your own pet subjects for research.

So – when a bookshop asks whether you have any remaindered copies of your book, they are really asking to buy them at a considerably reduced price. It must be your decision whether you should offer the remaining quarter of your print run at a lower price or to perhaps sell them more slowly at your originally determined full price.

## Should I write an autobiography?

If you are thinking of writing the story of your life with a view to it being accepted by a 'mainstream' publisher, the answer should probably be no. And the reason for that slight equivocation is the possibility that you may already be well-known – famous.

If a famous pop-star, media celebrity, footballer or politician were to approach a publisher with the offer of an autobiography they could well get an ecstatic welcome. (And they'd probably be using a 'ghost' to write their story – for more on which *see* later.) The public are ever avid readers of the life-stories of well-known people, but the autobiography of someone ordinary, like you or I – no way.

No matter how interesting or exciting you think your life has been, Joe Public doesn't want to know. You need to be famous first. Go off and swim the Atlantic under water or do something equally unique.

If, however, you can turn a short period of your life into something really funny, unusual, or different – but funny is best – you might be able to interest a publisher in a book about that. I know someone who wrote a very funny book about her one-year stint as a conductor, a 'clippie', on a bus; another friend has written about her college years and how she coped with her husband's new profession. She woke up one morning to find herself in bed with the vicar.

Mainstream publication is not the only end-result of an autobiography, though. The story of your early life will be of great interest to your children and on to their children's children. Life was different when you were young. So, by all means write down all you can remember about your life, get it onto paper, work on it as any writer should – make it readable. But don't expect a mainstream publisher to accept it; don't spend your hard-earned life-savings on having it published with a view to selling it yourself. Better, accept that it is just for the family.

If you have a word processor (*see* page 116), you can produce a handful of final copies of your autobiography in near-book form, interleaving illustrations perhaps, and have one or two copies properly bound. Lay it out and print the whole book to A5 size, rather than A4 – it'll look better. (You don't need a 'Desk-top Publishing' program – most of today's word processors will be perfectly adequate for the layout job needed.)

**I am in my 80s and have lived in the same town all my life. I have many memories of what it was like years ago – and I've started writing these down. Should I offer them, piecemeal, to the local newspaper, or should I pay to have them published privately?**

Other than a few copies for family and friends, I would strongly urge you not to pay for your memoirs to be published.

If you go to what is called a Vanity Publisher (*see* page 126), they will assure you that your story is fascinating and possibly a literary gem; then they'll take a lot of your money, produce your book as cheaply as possible and thereafter do little or nothing with it. You will be stuck with trying to sell a lot of badly produced books.

If you yourself arrange for a specialist printer to produce your book – understanding that you will have to do the 'publishing', i.e., you will self-publish your book (*see* page 127) – you will already have recognised that you are going to do all the selling. Either way, we come back to the harsh truth that there is no great demand for the autobiographies of us 'ordinary' folk.

So … as in the previous answer, I suggest you produce your own book – just a handful of copies – merely for family and friends.

Now, your other suggestion. It is possible that your local newspaper would be interested in your memories of long-ago local life. But – and it's a big but – your memories would need to be written to the newspaper's requirements rather than as for your intended book.

Almost certainly, the newspaper would want fairly short self-contained pieces. I would expect 500 words maximum – and 200 words would probably be better. They would undoubtedly have to be written in the style preferred by the newspaper – which could well mean short, 'tabloidy' sentences and paragraphs. And, yes, I know: it's much harder work 'writing short' than 'writing long'.

I suggest you write two or three short pieces and offer them, with the promise of more to come, to the editor of your local newspaper. Make a point of mentioning, in a covering letter, that you are offering them '... for consideration for publication *at your usual rates of payment*', so that the editor doesn't think they are for free. You could perhaps write each of your short pieces about a specific local place or street, or maybe about a specific trade – milkman, coalman, knife-sharpener, ice-cream vendor, etc.

Whatever the subject though, I suggest that your pieces have to be personalised – after all, the editor can reprint 50-year-old material from his own files. What you have to offer must be *different*.


**I am writing my autobiography. I've started by getting it all (about 70,000 words) down on the word-processor. I think of it as the first draft, but it's a hotch-potch of bits and pieces. How can I ORGANISE it all into a book?**

You've certainly started well, by getting it all down. That might be thought of as 'having done the research'. It's your *raw material*. And you are right to recognise that all that potentially valuable material has to be *organised*.

You can't reasonably expect to remember in detail all that you've written – all those 'bits and pieces'. So I think the first thing to do is to make a list of what you've got: list the content of each bit and piece – and give a date for each item in your list. You may think not, but you might well have remembered things slightly out of order. Check. Even though – *see* below – you may *organise* your recollections differently, you need to know when things actually happened.

Now perhaps you should stop and think about the end result you are aiming at. If you are famous or have done something really extraordinary, then maybe you can hope to sell your autobiography to a mainstream publisher. In my view, the only sensible alternative to that, is to produce just a few copies of your autobiography – for family and friends. I strongly urge you to avoid both the pitfalls of vanity publishers – who take anything – and all the non-writing effort of self-publishing.

So it's Fame or Family. And you need to consider and organise your material differently, depending on which of these is your route.

Not everyone will be interested in much 'ordinary' family history – who wore what at Auntie Mabel's wedding, who said what to whom when Grandad had his first ride in a motorcar. If you're famous, weed out such recollection-notes; if you're family-oriented, leave 'em in. If you're famous, maybe you should restrict what you include in your life story to events that have a bearing or relationship with the reason for your fame. Anyone reading the autobiography of a self-made millionaire wants to know how you did it and possibly not how much or little you enjoyed your school days. Great-grandson though will probably revel in the story of your dispute with the form teacher.

Whichever your end purpose – Fame or Family – you should investigate and apply the 'rules' for fiction-writing to your autobiography. Make it read like a well-crafted story.

You should *organise* the material in your autobiography around a consistent and ongoing theme. You should bring in bits of your story in such a way that, together, they fit into and form an identifiable plot or storyline. You should make sure that all the characters in your life story – including yourself, of course – really come alive. We all have 'warts': include them, they give realism. And when your characters are speaking, make sure they sound 'lifelike-only-better'; ensure that every speech moves the story forward. Search among your raw material for recollections of how you saw, felt about, revelled in the *places*, the settings of your scenes. Make sure that your recollections let the reader *experience* rather than just read. Fiction writing teachers repeatedly recommend 'Show, don't tell.'

And don't neglect to emphasise the problems that you faced – while delaying the explanation of how you overcame them. Throughout, wherever possible, hold back a punch-line. *'Make 'em laugh, make 'em cry, make 'em WAIT.'*

**A friend of mine is famous – but is not a writer. He has asked me to write the story of his life. What do I do first – negotiate with my friend or find a publisher? Should I write the story as a biography or as an autobiography? And, by the way, what is a *ghost*?**

Unless you are yourself an experienced and already published author, I think I would capitalise on your friend's fame and write his story as an autobiography. Let his name appear on the cover, not yours – his name will help the book to sell, yours would not. If he's really famous, he could get invited onto radio and/or TV chat shows, gaining publicity for the book that you could never attract.

Your authorial anonymity will make you a ghost. A ghost is just a 'behind-the-scenes' writer who writes someone else's story, 'as them'. Sometimes a ghost's name appears on the title page as 'with' the famous person. That may be something you need to negotiate with your friend.

Now the other matters. I suggest you talk it over – i.e. negotiate informally – with your friend first. You need to agree how the money will be split; how much time the friend will make available to you, to interview him; how much, and what, background and documentary material your friend will provide you with; and whether or not, and to what extent, your friend is to have an approval/veto role in respect of the final text. While discussing all of this informally, with your friend, make it clear that there will be no deal at all if you cannot sell the idea to a publisher before you start on it.

Once you and your friend are agreed informally on your working relationship, it will be up to you – as one who knows how the publishing world works – to find 'the right' publisher, sell him on the deal, and negotiate publishing terms. And although a literary agent is not always essential for some non-fiction books, the services of one will almost certainly be a major asset in the negotiations with publishers.

At this stage, it might be wise to formalise your relationship with your famous friend – an exchange of letters would be ideal. Informal, friendly agreements can sometimes unravel with time – and even quicker if and when the money gets bigger (or smaller) than expected.

## And finally...

Now that you've reached the end of the book, it's time to bite the bullet. There will always be more questions, fresh problems to solve - no one knows all the answers. What is really important is that you get on with your own writing. Apply bum to seat and pen to paper (or keyboard to screen, nowadays). Write something. Write anything. But write. Problems can be sorted out later.

**Recommended further reading**

*How To Write About Yourself,* Alison Chisholm and Brenda Courtie
(Allison & Busby, London, 1999.)
*How to Publish Yourself,* Peter Finch
(Allison & Busby, London, 1987 and 1997.)
*Marketing for Small Publishers,* Godber, Webb and Smith
(Journeyman Press, London, 1992.) Basically for small publishers and invaluable to self-publishers, this book will also help the author understand the publishing business.

# INDEX